What Makes Bread Rise?

What Makes Bread Rise?

A science-based weight loss program for America's families

Doug Kaufmann

with David Holland, M.D.

MediaTrition Inc.
Rockwall, Texas

Edited and produced by Chris Nygaard
intexdfw@yahoo.com

Published by MediaTrition
301 W. Washington Street
Rockwall, Texas 75807
(972)772-0990
knowthecause.com

First printing

Publisher's-Cataloguing-in-Publication
Provided by Quality Books, Inc.

Kaufmann, Doug A., 1949-
What Makes Bread Rise? : A science-based
weight loss program for America's families/
by Doug A. Kaufmann with David Holland

p. cm. -- (The fungus link series ; v. 3)
Includes bibliographical references and index.
ISBN 0-9703418-3-2

1. Obesity--Etiology. 2. Weight Loss.
3. Medical mycology. 4. Fungi 5. Weight loss
I. Holland, David A. II. Title

RC628.K365 2003   613.2'5
                       QBI03-200375

Manufactured in the United States of America

Title by Doug Kaufmann.

Cover (photo and design) by Chris Nygaard.

To the men, women
and children
who have suffered
through countless diets
and immeasurable
frustration.

Success lies
within your grasp.

Acknowledgments

Many thanks to my partner, Dr. David Holland, M.D. and our editor/book producer, Chris Nygaard, M.S., for another book well done. I must also thank Jami Clark, R.N. for her diligent proof-reading. Finally, thanks go to my wife, Ruth, my sons Evan and Ethan, and to Dave's wife Anny, his son Jacob and daughter Julia. Without your support, this book would not have been possible.

-Doug Kaufmann

Preface

Yeast! That's the answer to the question on the cover of this book. "Wait a minute," some of you are thinking. "I thought I bought a book that's supposed to show me a new approach to slimming down. Whether yeast makes bread rise or not has absolutely nothing to do with weight loss."

In fact, yeast and other microscopic fungi that often contaminate grains and other food staples are *intricately connected* with weight gain. This will become clear as you read the following chapters on fungi, the toxins they make, and how these microscopic pathogens are likely affecting your health even as you read these words.

Toward the back of this book, you will find the Kaufmann Antifungal program that literally thousands of people have used to achieve good health. If you have any questions, please don't hesitate to call my office at 972-772-0990. Dr. Holland practices medicine in in the Dallas Fort Worth Metroplex. You can reach him at 817-861-4100. Finally, our website is www.knowthecause.com.

Good luck,
-Doug Kaufmann

Kaufmann and Holland

Table of Contents

Part I
Know the Cause

Part II
Life-style Change

*If
you always
do what you've
always done....
You'll always get
what you've
always got.*

-Doug Kaufmann

Kaufmann and Holland

Part One
Know the Cause

• •

Introduction
Fight fungi, lose weight and live longer

Losing weight will do a lot more than give you an opportunity to shop for new clothes in smaller sizes. Recent studies show that slimming down could actually add 20 years to your life. You would decrease your risks of developing diabetes, heart disease, cancer and arthritis[1] — and you would lower your chances of having a baby with birth defects.[2]

Weight loss could even help us at the national level. Tired of hearing about the overburdened, American health care system? Consider this — in terms of related medical conditions and expenses, excess weight costs our nation more money than *smoking* does.[3,4] Just think — if we could lose enough weight and stop smoking, we could both save social security and make sure every man, woman and child in America had access to adequate health care!

Despite these powerful motivators, the number of overweight or obese Americans has risen past the 60 percent mark, with no stopping point in sight. That means that, whether you are standing in line at the post office or shopping at the supermarket, two out of every three of the people there with you have traded years of their lives for inches around the waistline.

Weight problems have also affected our children. Fully one in five are overweight now.[5] Childhood obesity comes with more than just a price tag for baggier and baggier clothes and the threat of problems later on in life. For example, although type 1 diabetes used to be called "juvenile," while type 2 diabetes was termed "adult onset," half of the kids diagnosed with the disease today are developing *type 2* diabetes.

Let's back up for a moment. Half the battle in problem solving is defining what the problem is in the first place. You just read that by losing weight, we can both live longer and healthier lives and save a great deal on medical bills. But does that mean that fat actually shortens life?

In fact, it doesn't mean that at all. By way of analogy, picture that just after your optometrist informs you that you need bifocals, your hair falls out. It is highly unlikely that your failing eyesight has somehow damaged your hair follicles. A third factor — age, a vitamin deficiency, stress or a hormonal dysfunction — has likely caused both problems. To return to our discussion, although blaming fat cells and molecules for cancer, diabetes and arthritis may seem the thing to do, logic dictates that another factor may be at work. If we could take care of that unknown factor, it makes sense that we could both knock out obesity and the diseases that have become associated with it.

Certainly, it's a snap to see that failing eyesight doesn't make hair fall out. But it's not so easy to raise the question as to whether fat cells really cause diabetes, cancer and birth defects. Why is that?

I think one reason is that, compared to other tissues, fat looks inherently *evil*. We associate it with laziness. We're even a tad suspicious when health care professionals talk about "good" fats. How could there be anything *good* about fat?

As it turns out, fat is how our bodies store energy. It is an essential part of the walls that surround the billions of cells that make us who we are. And, it insulates our organs from injury and serves as padding for our joints and ligaments. Finally, were we to cut what are called the essential fatty acids from our diets, we would get sick and die.

So, if fat cells are not inherently deadly, why does losing weight prolong life? If Dr. Holland and I are right, it isn't the weight loss that deserves the credit, but rather the steps that we take to lose the weight in the first place. Things such as exercise and eating a low carb diet rich in fiber do more than just take off the pounds and inches — they count as two steps we can take to protect ourselves from microscopic fungi and their toxins.

At least with regard to birth defects, mothers' weight problems are clearly not to blame. When children are born with birth defects, doctors almost always find that their DNA has been damaged in some way. I have yet to see any evidence that connects fat with the damage in question. On the other hand, an abundance of literature points to the roles of fungi and their toxins in causing not just the DNA damage responsible for birth defects, but cancer, heart disease, diabetes and yes, even weight gain.

Many people continue to believe that advances in technology and nutrition will eventually make obesity a thing of the past. I used to be the same way. In fact, knowledge of gains made here and there in the world of science often seems to displace common sense about what we should be eating, and the life-styles we should be pursuing. Low-fat advocates fight tooth and nail with low-carb proponents. Conventional medicine battles with alternative medicine. And all the while our children grow fatter, our lives are shortened and we suffer from diseases and disabilities that we should have been able to figure out how to avoid by now.

Dr. Holland and I have watched some of the latest developments in diet plans with great interest. As a country, we do seem to be making progress. Low-carb regimens such as the Atkins diet are enjoying increased recognition, even in the face of criticism from mainstream medical and dietician groups. But I should warn you — even though low carb diets do work, because they miss the point as to why avoiding carbohydrates is a good idea, they are not the best plans you could follow.

Carbohydrates encompass both simple sugars — table sugar, for example — and the complex sugars that make up the bulk of grains and pastas. Some scientists maintain that overeating carbohydrates leads to a condition called insulin resistance, which in turn causes weight gain. The fact is, the whole problem with carbohydrates, in and of themselves, may have less to do with insulin resistance and a lot more to do with a problem that farmers battle on a regular basis — the fungal contamination of grains.

In this book, Dr. Holland and I zero in on the cause of weight gain. We then show you what course of action you need to take to slim down and stay that way. We start our discussion in the next chapter with vital information as to what exactly these fungi and mycotoxins are, and how it is that they cause disease.

1. Mercola.com 2003.

2. Mercola.com, 2003. Obesity and diabetes increases risk of birth defects- citing Epidemiology, Nov 2000;11:689-694).

3. Wall Street Journal, March 2003.

4. Mercola, citing an article in Public Health, June 2001;115:229-235.

5. Boyles, S. WebMD Medical News. WebMD.com. March 13, 2002).

Kaufmann and Holland

Chapter 2
Toward an understanding of fungi and fungal disease

This chapter presents an overview of fungi, their role in our world, and how they can cause human diseases. For contrasts and comparisons, let's start with a quick look at some of the characteristics that define plants, animals and fungi as distinct from one another.

The Three Kingdoms

The Plant Kingdom

Green plants contain chlorophyll, which enables them to combine energy from the sun, nitrogen from the soil, carbon dioxide from the air and hydrogen from water in order to make energy. Plants release oxygen in the process, and they store their energy in the form of sugar, another name for which is *carbohydrate*.

Trees turn various colors in the fall because their leaves have lost all their chlorophyll, which in turn reveals other pigments that had been hidden. Without chlorophyll, plants are forced to stop growing and to subsist on the energy they have stored until the following spring. It is because growth stops and starts in this way that we are able to measure the age of a tree stump by counting its rings.

The Animal Kingdom

When animals eat plants, they ingest the sun's energy, once removed (in the form of carbohydrate), along with other substances such as fibers and oils. This energy is easily digested and put to use for cell functions such as fashioning proteins from amino acids. Energy not used is stored as fat. When animals eat other animals, they ingest not only the fat — the sun's energy twice removed — but tissues such as protein-rich muscle, as well. Because these tissues are at least twice removed from the original energy of the sun, they require more time and different mechanisms to break them down than do the pure carbohydrates gotten from plants.

The Kingdom of Fungi

Because fungi lack chlorophyll and cannot move to stalk their prey, instead of creating energy by assembling ingredients from sun, soil, air and water, they break down existing plant and animal matter into carbohydrate, or sugar, which they then absorb for their own use. Components besides carbohydrates that fungi do not use are then made available to green plants. The life cycle then begins all over again.

Yeasts, molds, mildew, smuts and rusts are all forms and species of fungi. Without them, debris from dead plants and animals would pile up by the tons. The energy and nutrients collected from sun and soil would remain unavailable for sustaining new life.

Although we typically picture this kind of breakdown as happening to a fallen tree — or to us after we've been buried six feet underground — as a matter of fact, fungi are by their very nature constantly working to break down even living things, including us. In other words, to be alive and healthy means to be actively antifungal, while the absence of adequate defenses against fungal invasion and infection leads to illness and death.

Scientists who study fungi are called mycologists. They tell us that the number of fungal species identified so far is approaching 100,000, and they estimate that more than 1.5 million have yet to be recognized.[3,4]

Fungi range from the edible and even delicious puffballs and truffles to the deadly *Mucor* group of molds that can invade and kill a human in a matter of hours. They can vary in size from less than a micron across for a single yeast spore, to mushrooms the size of a man, to woodland mold colonies that measure hundreds of acres across.

Yeasts are single-cell organisms, whereas molds and mushrooms are groups of cells clustered together. Fungi in general can reproduce either sexually — by sharing DNA, dividing and growing — or asexually, by releasing spores into the environment that go on to form new, adult fungi or by budding new yeast cells from a parent cell.

The spores released from a single mushroom can number in the trillions, and they are so resilient that they can survive intact for thousands of years, until such time that the temperature, moisture content, and food supply is adequate to allow germination into the adult form once again.

Fungal cells compared to human cells

Fungal cells are similar to human cells in that they not only contain a nucleus — that is, a command center that both contains the cell's genetic material and regulates activity for the entire cell — but they also share many of the same pathways required for growth and reproduction. In fact, fungi are more closely related to human cells in terms of function and genetics than either viruses or bacteria.[6] A bacteria cell has no nucleus at its center, while a virus is best characterized as a naked, opportunistic package of DNA.

One of the primary differences between single-celled fungi and human cells is that fungi have rigid cell walls much like those found in plants, while human cells are instead surrounded and protected by flexible, cell membranes. Many of the prescription, antifungal drugs have been designed to kill or disable microscopic fungi by attacking this cell wall. Focus on this characteristic enables scientists to avoid killing the human cell at the same time. Still, fungi's similarity to human cells can pose a challenge to drug researchers in that it is often difficult to design or isolate chemicals that will selectively kill the fungus, but spare the human.

Thus far, about 400 species of microscopic fungi have been found to be capable of infecting people.[13] Of these, fewer than 100 are routinely identified as having infected human patients.

The difficulty of diagnosing fungal illness

Fungal cells' similarity to human cells can make the proper diagnosis of a fungal infection quite difficult. Without the use of proper isolation and staining techniques by microbiologists and pathologists, doctors can often fail to properly identify fungal pathogens. Microscopic fungi can be confused with both normal human blood cells and even malignant cancer cells,[7] which can lead to profoundly incorrect courses of treatment. You could be prescribed an antibiotic for a "bacterial" infection when your condition actually calls for an antifungal drug.

In such cases, antibiotics often actually make the fungus-infected patient sicker because they destroy the friendly bacteria in the intestines. Again, the yeast overgrowth that occurs in these bacteria's absence can cause all kinds of medical problems. As their patients' conditions worsen, doctors often deduce — for all the wrong reasons — that the antibiotic they prescribed was inappropriate. "Must have been a resistant bug," they decide. "Let's try a stronger, or maybe a different antibiotic." What many doctors tend not to consider is that maybe their patients are not suffering from a bacterial infection, at all.

Misdiagnosis of fungal infections can lead to much more serious consequences. In the worst-case scenario, physicians not trained to identify fungal disease can instead misinterpret X-rays of fungus-infected lesions as actually indicating the presence of cancer. The pathologists who receive tissue work-ups of lesions from such physicians are trained to find cancer cells — they, as well, have not been adequately trained how to recognize cells sickened by fungal toxins or spores.[8,9] In many cases, misdiagnosis is no one's fault at this stage. As Dr. John Rex, M.D. says, "There are no rapid, accurate diagnostic tests that can confirm with certainty the presence of invasive fungal disease."

In this way, cancer can be incorrectly diagnosed. Ironically, because the ensuing chemotherapy is toxic to fungi, as well as to cancerous cells, a reverse of the progress of the infection reinforces physicians' conviction that the diagnosis of cancer was correct. If and when the fungal infection does eventually come to their attention, they tend to interpret it as a secondary illness of the type commonly found in chemotherapy-weakened patients. In more than one case, surgeons have removed growths they had thought were cancerous, only to discover that the growth in question was actually a fungal infection. Although surgery was perhaps the course needed in either case, had the fungal nature of the disease been known more in advance, quite likely the procedure could have been avoided.

The point is, if you are diagnosed with cancer, as soon as possible you should take steps to investigate whether your condition may have been caused by an infection by microscopic fungi, or through exposure to the mycotoxins that fungi produce. For more on this, please see our book, *The Germ That Causes Cancer*.

The danger of ignoring mycotoxins
Another problem with medical mycology — the study of fungi-caused disease — is that mycologists may be spending too much time researching pathogens that infect us directly, and not enough time on the dangers we face from the toxins produced by all fungi. These "mycotoxins" are capable of causing a wide variety of health problems.

Although agricultural mycologists admit the damage that mycotoxins in contaminated grain feeds or grasses can cause to livestock, medical mycologists minimize the danger of these mycotoxins to the *people* who eat many of the same grains. It would be better for everyone concerned if the scientists from these two fields could share data with one another every now and then.

According to the American Cancer Society, "Mycotoxins are genotoxic carcinogens, and exposure begins in utero and in mother's milk, continuing throughout life; these conditions favor the occurrence of disease." -*American Cancer Society Textbook of Clinical Oncology.*[15]

Mycotoxins are heat-stable chemicals produced by fungi that contaminate grains such as corn, wheat, barley, and sorghum. "Heat stable" means that you can't destroy them simply by cooking the grains they have contaminated. Mycotoxins can have various effects on humans and animals, ranging from benign and beneficial to debilitating and deadly.

Fungi owe much of the credit for their own survival to these mycotoxins, in that the chemicals kill off or limit the growth of competing germs such as bacteria. To varying degrees, mycotoxins suppress the immune systems of infected hosts — livestock or humans, for example — so that the fungus producing the toxins avoids the defensive reactions it would normally face from its hosts. Mycotoxins can even damage human DNA, a process that can lead to cancer. An important example of this is seen in the liver cancer caused by aflatoxin, an *Aspergillus* mold toxin that initiates very specific breaks in human DNA strands. Aflatoxin exposure has been associated with genetic mutations such as the p53 gene mutation seen in more than half of all human cancers.[16]

To sum up, consumption or inhalation of small amounts of mycotoxins can lead to problems such as bacterial infections or even cancer. These conditions are often diagnosed and treated, while the underlying cause — immune system suppression or alteration of genetic codes due to mycotoxins in the body — goes unrecognized. That said, mycotoxin levels occasionally rise dramatically enough that the poisons are recognized as the cause of a given condition. For example, in the United States between 1997 and 1998, 1,700 children became ill when they ate burritos contaminated with vomitoxin (deoxynivalenol).[17] Vomitoxin is a major contaminant of grains such as wheat, barley and corn that have been infested with *Fusarium* molds.[18] These grains are vulnerable to fungal contamination any time during the growing season, harvest and storage processes.

Infection paths

Fungi can invade our bodies via a number of routes. Their spores lace the air we breathe. Construction projects can liberate fungal spores from deep in the soil, after which such spores are carried far and wide by the wind. The wind can also transport fungal spores from their native soils to regions far away.[12] Fungi and their toxins often contaminate staple grains such as corn, thereby entering our food supply and becoming a problem to both livestock and humans. Sexual transmission of yeast infections also remains a very real problem, and one that often seems to go overlooked by medical personnel.[11] Finally, homes flooded or damaged by water are prime targets for a wide range of fungi. This puts occupants at risk of inhaling both the spores and toxins that such fungi produce.

The upshot is that any mysterious illness or disease of unknown origin, whether you were previously in perfect health or ill with a chronic disease like cancer or diabetes, should prompt you and your doctor to consider whether you may have been exposed to fungi in one of the manners described above. For more on this, please see the Fungal Quotient Questionnaire at the back of this book.

The truth about antibiotics

Most antibiotics are actually mycotoxins. Penicillin counts as perhaps the most famous example. A scientist named Alexander Fleming discovered the mycotoxin in 1928, when bacteria cultures he was growing were accidentally contaminated by the fungus that produces penicillin — *Penicillium*. Circular gaps appeared around each of the fungus colonies that grew on Fleming's plate, within which bacteria failed to grow, despite the absence of any fungus cells. These gaps were due to penicillin's antibiotic powers. Fleming determined that the *Penicillium* mold spores that contaminated his bacterial plates had originated in a decaying orange one floor above his lab, and that they had entered his lab through a window he'd left open.

Several years passed before penicillin was isolated and then mass-produced. Refinements and laboratory-induced mutations have led to the enhanced versions of *Penicillium* molds we have today. Current strains of *Penicillium* used in commercial, pharmaceutical settings are 10,000 times as efficient as Fleming's original, laboratory sample.[19]

Antibiotics gave medicine a huge boost. For the first time, doctors could actually cure what had been deadly, bacterial infections. That said, scientists such as Dr. John Pitt, remain skeptical as to their true value. "It is ironic that this humbled fungus, hailed as a benefactor of mankind," Dr. Pitt writes, "may by its very success prove to be a deciding factor in the decline of the present civilization."[21]

Norman F. Conant, lead author of a book entitled the *Manual of Clinical Mycology*, also warns about the side effects of antibiotic use. "Fungus infections," he writes, "are relatively, if not actually, more frequent in occurrence since the introduction of penicillin and other potent antibiotics for the control of the acute bacterial diseases."[20]

With the rise in cancer and autoimmune diseases, and the all-to-common and ever-increasing use of antibiotics since the 1950s, you have to wonder if we aren't making a mistake. After all, a number of scientists have thoroughly documented the link between mycotoxins and cancer. As well, several side effects associated with antibiotics and other drugs derived from fungi actually mimic the signs and symptoms of autoimmune dysfunction. In some cases, you could even say that adverse reactions to antibiotic use qualify as "mycotoxicoses." Mycotoxicosis, the singular form of the word, is defined as an identifiable illness caused by a fungally produced poison.

Beyond antibiotics

Other drugs derived from fungi include cholesterol-lowering "statin" drugs made by *Aspergillus terreus* and other molds.[22] Fungi are also used to produce Cephalosporin antibiotics, antifungals such as griseofulvin and nystatin, chemotherapeutics (adriamycin, dactinomycin, etc.), and immune-suppressing drugs such as cyclosporin. With the low cost involved in maintaining and culturing them, balanced against their enormous yield of expensive drugs, fungi are the most profitable organisms in the world. At the same time, as a class they count as the most destructive — an estimated 80 percent of annual crop losses worldwide involve either fungal contamination, or outright destruction wreaked by fungi.

Other fungal toxins

Because it is a fermentation by-product of a yeast called *Saccharo-myces cerevisiae*, alcohol counts as a mycotoxin in all of its many forms. A number of beers and wines are also made with the help of other fungi, including *Aspergillus* species.[24] These fungi in turn make their own mycotoxins that can contaminate the final batch of wine or beer. On top of that, grains unfit for use as breakfast cereals or pastas — deemed so in part because of their excessive mycotoxin content — are often used instead for making alcoholic beverages.[25]

The upshot is that alcoholism is one of the more prevalent forms of mycotoxicosis. In both the short and long run, alcohol can cause mental impairments and aberrations, scarring of and fatty deposits in the liver, and more than 50 different types of cancer.[23] Unfortunately, the mycotoxin's protective effects, as indicated by recent studies, have come to overshadow these long-term concerns. A glass of wine a day may very well bring short-term health benefits with it, but if it *kills* you in the long run, the original benefits are hardly worth the effort and expense.

Aspergillus niger produces citric acid very efficiently, an ability that commercial food producers put to use — to the tune of more 350 kilotons a year. The majority of this citric acid — again, a myc-otoxin — is used as a preservative in products such as soft drinks. It is perhaps no coincidence that calcium loss through urination has been linked to the caffeine or acids that sodas contain.[26] The loss can lead to osteoporosis.

Speaking of osteoporosis, other mycotoxins besides citric acid can interfere with normal calcium function in the body. CPA — cyclopiazonic acid — counts among them. Chickens who eat grains contaminated with this chemical produce fragile, thin-shelled eggs because the acid has bound up the calcium needed to form normal eggs.[27] CPA is made by *Aspergillus flavus* and can be found in cheese (particularly in camembert), peanuts, and millet, among other products.

Since the fructose syrup used as sweeteners in soft drinks comes mainly from corn — the grain most commonly infested by *Aspergillus flavus* — sugar-sweetened sodas represent one of the major routes by which Americans may be ingesting CPA. This development might explain the recent osteoporosis epidemic.

Zearalenone is an estrogen-like mycotoxin made by the *Fusarium* species of mold. High grain contamination rates by this toxin have been reported in Canada, the U.S. and northern Europe.[28] The paper containing this information also estimates the daily intake of zearalenone by Canadians at 1.2 micrograms per person. This relatively low dose increases for people who eat more corn products. The effects of low-dose exposures to these toxins over a period of many years — the primary concern of many scientists in the field of mycotoxicology — have yet to be determined.

Zearalenone has mostly been studied in farm animals. Its effects range from infertility, swelling and enlargement of female genitalia and mammary glands, problems with ovulation, menstrual irregularities, fetal miscarriage, and feminization of male animals, with pigs being affected the most. In addition, some scientists suspect zearalenone as a cause of premature puberty in girls and of cervical cancer in women.[29]

Tremorgen mycotoxins such as penitrem A are made by *Aspergillus*, *Penicillium* and other mold species. These toxins can cause tremors, headaches, fever and dementia in animals and humans. Other neurotoxic mycotoxins include vomitoxin and the T-2 mycotoxin. Both are made by *Fusarium* species, and both can cause nerve damage, anorexia (feed refusal in animals), vomiting, bloody diarrhea, and a weakened immune system.[30] Vomitoxin typically contaminates grains that have been infected with *Fusarium* molds.[31] Mycotoxins such as vomitoxin and T-2 are much more dangerous when inhaled than when eaten in contaminated food.[32] This makes them of primary concern in enclosed, mold-infested places such as grain silos, office buildings and homes.

Together with vomitoxin, *Aspergillus*-and-*Penicillium*-produced ochratoxin A has also been connected with various forms of kidney damage. Even in "naturally occurring levels," both mycotoxins can damage the kidneys of humans and animals."[33]

Inadequate limits
The FDA has set limits for allowable levels of aflatoxin in finished foods intended for human or livestock consumption. Milk and grain products destined for the table cannot exceed 0.5 parts per billion (ppb) and 20 ppb, respectively. If we assume that most farmers produce milk and grow grains that contain close to these allowable limits, then Americans ingest between 0.15 and 0.5 mg of aflatoxin — the most carcinogenic substance known to science — on a daily basis.

Livestock feed is allowed to contain up to 300 ppb of aflatoxin. Again assuming that most farmers use feed that contains close to this allowed limit, even if only a small percentage of the mycotoxin makes it from animals' intestines into their tissues, and from there onto our tables and into our stomachs, 300 ppb is very likely an unacceptably high level of contamination.

The FDA screens crops for only aflatoxin, even though Food and Drug Administration samples have proved that other toxins contaminate American-grown grains.[35] Although screening programs in the United States have been set for one or two other toxins, compliance programs have yet to be executed. Some countries screen for as many as eight of the most common mycotoxins on a regular basis. That said, as of 2002 on the international level, only 77 countries had reported that they regulate mycotoxins in foods and feeds. Thirteen countries reported no regulations whatsoever.

The Future

Mycotoxicoses represent an area of relatively new study. Although ergotism from the ergot toxin was suspected as the cause in St. Anthony's Fire way as early as the middle ages, carcinogenic aflatoxin was not discovered until 1960, and the fumonisin toxins, implicated as the cause of human esophageal cancer, were only identified in 1988.[37] Even so, mycotoxins and the problems they cause — let alone the fungi themselves — are seldom if ever studied by physicians. According to a scientist in Croatia, "Mycotoxicoses are usually insufficiently taught in medical textbooks and are not covered in curricula of many medical schools."[36] This statement pretty much describes American schools, as well.

Any honest look at why our rates of cancer, obesity, Alzheimer's, diabetes and other chronic, debilitating diseases have recently gone through the roof should take into consideration our consumption of these cancer-and-other disease-causing chemicals on a daily basis through our grain-heavy diets. That said, a mycotoxin-free diet is actually unrealistic. In other words, any diet designed to minimize ingestion of fungi and their mycotoxins must also contain plenty of antifungals to combat those microbes and toxins that will inevitably make it through, despite our best intentions. The antifungal program detailed toward the back of the book satisfies both of these criteria.

1. Lawrence, E.; Harniess, S., An Instant Guide to Mushrooms and other Fungi. Crescent Books, New York. 1991.

21. Hellinghausen, M., *Fungal infections pose danger.* Nurseweek. 22 April 1996.

3. Moore-Landecker., *Fundamentals of the Fungi,* 4th ed. Prentice-Hall, Inc. New Jersey. 1996; Mycotoxins: Risks in Plant, Animal, and Human Systems.

4. *Mycotoxins: Risks in Plant, Animal, and Human Systems.* Council for Agricultural Science and Technology Task Force Report No. 139. Ames, Iowa. Jan 2003. www.cast-science.org.

5. Conant, et al., *Manual of Clinical Mycology.* 2nd ed. WB Saunders Co. Philadelphia, 1954.

6. http://hsc.virginia.edu/med-ed/micro/myc/myc1.html, 2003.

7. Mattman, L. 1993. Cell wall deficient forms: Stealth Pathogens.

8. Kibbler, C.C. Principles and Practice of Medical Mycology. Wiley. West Sussex, England. 1996.

9. Kaufmann, C. *Nonresolving pneumonia: Is endemic mycosis to blame?* The Journal of Respiratory Disease, Vol 16, No. 11, Nov 1995.

10. Managing fungal infections in the new millennium. Medscape.com. 4/2000.

11. Kibbler, C.C., *Principles and Practice of Medical Mycology.* Wiley. West Sussex, England. 1996.

12. Lin, J., Hamill, R. *Coccidioidomycosis Pulmonary Infection.* Current Infectious Disease Reports 2001,3:274-278.

13. Kibbler.

14. Burrow, W.W.B., Textbook of Microbiology; Saunders Co., Philadelphia, 1959.

15. Murphy, G.P. et. al. American Cancer Society Textbook of Clinical Oncology., 2nd. Ed. 1995. American Cancer Society, Inc. Atlanta, GA.

16. Lane, K., *Aflatxoin, tobacco, ammonia and the p53 tumor-suppressor gene: cancer's missing link?* Medscape General Medicine 1(2). Medscape Portals, Inc. Aug 30, 1999.

17. Etzel, R. *Mycotoxins*. JAMA. Vol 287, No 4. Jan 23/30. 2002.

18. CAST 2003.

19. Moore-Landecker., Fundamentals of the Fungi, 4th ed. Prentice-Hall, Inc. New Jersey. 1996.

20. Conant, et al. Manual of Clinical Mycology. 2nd ed. WB Saunders Co. Philadelphia, 1954.

21. Pitt, J. The Genus Penicillium, Academic Press, 1979.

22. Physicians' Desk Reference. 48th edition. Medical Economics Data Production Company. Montvale, NJ. 1994.

23. Costantini, A.V., et al. Prevention of Breast Cancer: Hope at Last. Fungalbionics Series - The fungal/mycotoxin etiology of human disease. Johann Friedrich Oberlin Verlag. Germany. 1998. http://members.aol.com/jfoverlag/fungalbionics/.

24. Moore-Landecker., Fundamentals of the Fungi, 4th ed. Prentice-Hall, Inc. New Jersey. 1996.

25. CAST. Mycotoxins: economic and health risks. Report No. 116. Nov. 1989. Ames, IA.

26. Heaney, RP and Rafferty, K: Carbonated beverages and urinary calcium excretion. American Journal of Clinical Nutrition. 2001; 74.

27. CAST 2003.

28. Krska, R. Mycotoxins of growing interest: Zearalenone. Third Joint FAO/WHO/UNEP International Conference on Mycotoxins. Tunis, Tunisia, 3-6 March. 1999)

29. CAST 2003; Peraica, M., et al. Toxic effects of mycotoxins in humans. Bulletin of the World Health Organization. Sept 1, 1999.

30. CAST 2003.

31. Ibid.

32. Peraica, M., et al. Toxic effects of mycotoxins in humans. Bulletin of the World Health Organization. Sept 1, 1999.

33. CAST 2003.

34. Jay M. Arena, MD. Poisonings. 5th ed. 1986. Charles C. Thomas. Springfield, IL.

35. CAST 2003.

36. Peraica, M., toxicologist, Unit of Toxicology, Institute for Medical Research and Occupations Health Ksaverska cesta 2, POB 291, HR-1001 Sagreb, Croatia, et al. Toxic effects of mycotoxins in humans.

37. CAST 2003

Chapter 3
Why you should avoid
fungal growth promoters

In this chapter, Dr. Holland and I will address how farmers use antibiotics and other chemicals produced by fungi to promote faster and higher weight gain in their livestock. We will then apply this knowledge to strengthening the connection made in chapter two between doctor-prescribed antibiotics and weight gain in people, with a quick look at what we can do to prevent such weight gain. Finally, we will investigate the possibility that the beef and lamb at the supermarket remains contaminated by a percentage of the antibiotics and hormones fed to livestock, and what we should do based on this possibility.

Agricultural scientist TLJ Lawrence tells us that feeding antibiotics to livestock has generated an "almost miraculous" jump in how much and how fast the animals gain weight.[1] Antibiotics aren't the only growth promoter available to farmers today. To "improve" them physiologically, livestock are also fed growth hormones, stimulants and tranquilizers. And, adding enzymes and clay materials to feed allows farmers to manipulate how animals absorb nutrients from their food.[2]

Antibiotics and weight gain

How did the livestock antibiotic industry get its start? Lawrence tells us that in 1949 — around the time that antibiotics became a mainstay in medicine — the fungus *Streptomyces aureofaciens* was commonly used to ferment various substances. A scientist named Stockstad noticed that animals fed feed mixed with by-products produced by this fungus tended to put on more weight than animals fed standard feed. The following year, Lawrence and a colleague observed that livestock also gained weight more rapidly when they were fed fungi used in the manufacture of antibiotics — including *Streptomyces aureofaciens* — for human use. Scientists concluded that the fermentation byproducts produced by this and other fungi — antibiotics, in other words — were responsible for the weight gain in question.[3]

Within three years of this understanding, the British government had issued the "Therapeutic Substances Act," which allowed farmers free rein to include antibiotics in their animals' diets. From then until 1999, feeding antibiotics to livestock became a virtually worldwide practice.

In 1999, the European Community passed a ban on the use of antibiotics and other growth promoters in cattle, pigs, and poultry. The ban is set to take effect in 2006. It is based upon worries concerning the growing numbers of antibiotic-resistant bacteria, and the possibility that resistant bacteria from the intestines of animals could make it into our food supply.[4] Despite the ban in Europe, more than half of the antibiotics produced in North America continue to be used as growth promoters in livestock.[5]

Scientists have yet to completely understand the connection between antibiotics and livestock growth.[6] We do know that antibiotics can wipe out the bacteria that normally live in the intestines of these animals. Some scientists believe that because such bacteria require food, their absence — thanks to the antibiotics — frees up more food for digestion by the animal itself. In apparent support of this notion, when laboratory livestock whose intestines had been sterilized were fed antibiotics, they failed to gain any more weight.[7]

Although this theory looks good on paper, it fails in practice. It turns out that laboratory livestock whose intestines have been sterilized of all microbes tend to get sick more often, weigh much less than their normal counterparts and die much sooner. To counter the above theory, this likely happens because sterilized animals have been robbed of their friendly, intestinal bacteria. Although these friendly microbes do consume a limited number of calories, they also aid in the digestion of food, and they prevent disease-causing bacteria, viruses and fungi from gaining footholds in the intestines. In other words, their presence constitutes a net gain in nutritional and health benefits for their hosts.

Scientists of the "animals free of intestinal microbes get more calories from their food" camp are likely not only ignorant of the digestive help that friendly bacteria provide — they also neglect to consider the roles played by other, intestinal microbes such as the yeast, *Candida albicans*. Normally, the numbers of such microbes are held in check by friendly bacteria. When antibiotics wipe out these bacteria, yeasts and other fungi enjoy a population explosion that can have dire consequences for their hosts. One of those consequences is dramatic weight gain — a positive development only if you happen to be a livestock farmer. To recap, Dr. Holland

and I believe that animals with sterilized intestines fail to respond to antibiotics by growing faster because the yeasts and other fungi that can cause the increase in weight have already been removed from the picture.

The arguments laid out above apply to human weight gain, as well. In other words, patients prescribed antibiotics by their doctors stand a much higher risk of becoming obese. The question is, how much we are exposed to antibiotics during the course of our lives?

In answer to this, a recent paper maintains that 94 percent of American children are diagnosed at least once with an inner ear infection called acute otitis media (AOM) before they reach the age of two.[8] These infections generated 24.5 million office visits in 1990, up from 9.9 million in 1975. Doctors prescribe antibiotics for 96 percent of the ear infection patients they see, which ultimately translates to 24 million prescriptions a year.

You should know that, despite what has become general practice, it is not at all clear that inner ear infections call for antibiotics. In fact, some 80 percent of patients who don't take antibiotics end up quickly recovering with no medical intervention whatsoever. And, in one study of ear infection patients who took a popular antibiotic called Amoxicillin, the control group of patients who took no antibiotics at all actually got better faster.[9]

Still, if antibiotics pose zero health risks, then prescribing them for cases such as ear infections only makes sense. After all, if your child turns out to be a case that requires intervention, it would have been better if she'd taken antibiotics from the beginning of her illness.

Unfortunately, antibiotics are nothing if not risky. Not surprisingly, scientists have found that, in the antibiotic-deluged world of the present-day, yeast infections in babies have become a bigger problem than ever before.[10] Studies confirming a cause and effect relationship between antibiotics and intestinal yeast overgrowth include Keefer (1951), Childs (1956), Sklar (1961), Gram (1956), Campbell/Heseltine (1960), Cormane/Gosling (1963) and Tewari (1966). Tewari has said that "it has been *clearly established* that overgrowth of *Candida albicans* occurs [upon taking antibiotics]." In addition to the wide number of diseases that an overgrowth of yeast and other fungi can cause, any parent who gives his children antibiotics also puts them at risk for weight gain.

Of course, ear infections constitute only the tip of the proverbial iceberg when it comes to the use of antibiotics. For another example, across the country in most urgent care centers that treat adults, sinusitis is the most common disease being diagnosed today. Doctors prescribe antibiotics for most of these cases, as well.

To sum up, the rise we've seen in antibiotic consumption has not only led to resistant, superstrains of bacteria. It has directly contributed to the obesity epidemic in our country, as well.

Parents should be especially careful about giving antibiotics to babies. Scientists have found that infants who put on a great deal of weight in the first several months of life tend to grow up to be obese adults.[11] So, please do everything you can to protect your children from illnesses such as ear infections. Ways to do this include giving them the immune system boost that only breast-feeding can provide, and washing their hands and faces often. If your children do come down with ear aches, please give them a chance to heal on their own before you resort to antibiotics. At the same time, rememeber to stay in close contact with your family physician.

How to counteract the antibiotic effect

At the very least, after you finish taking a round of antibiotics, you should replace the friendly bacteria that the prescribed drug has killed off. You can do so by taking what is called a probiotic. Probiotics are supplements that deliver new colonies of friendly bacteria to your intestines.

Ideally, if you feel you must take an antibiotic, you should also ask your doctor to prescribe nystatin along with it. Nystatin is a topical antifungal. As a powder or cream, it is used for fungal (yeast) infections on the skin. In liquid form, lozenge or pill, it is used to treat oral, intestinal and vaginal yeast and fungal infections.*

We cannot emphasize enough that most of the antibiotics that farmers use as growth promoters have been derived from fungi — they are mycotoxins.

Hormonal growth promoters and weight gain

In addition to our discussion on antibiotic use in livestock, we should also look into farmers' practice of using *hormones* as growth

---

*Nystatin was developed in the early 1950s by two researchers. When it first came on the market in 1954, it was specifically indicated and prescribed for "the prevention and treatment of intestinal candidiasis, its use being indicated for patients treated with oral antibiotics, especially when the treatment was intensive or protracted."[12] Although nystatin cream is commonly prescribed today for skin infections such as diaper rash, USP Drug guidelines do not currently recommend its use internally for any one, specific disease. This means that you may have some difficulty convincing your doctor to prescribe nystatin tablets for you.[13] For more information, please see the chapter on prescription antifungals, located in *Supporting Materials*.

promoters. Hormones popular for promoting weight gain include estradiol, melengestrol acetate, progesterone, testosterone, trenbolone acetate and zeranol. Zeranol is a commercial form of zearalenone, a toxin produced by a fungus called *Fusarium*. This chemical stimulates animals' pituitary glands to produce more of a growth hormone called somatotropin.[14] Zeranol can also mimic the hormone estrogen,[15] the importance of which we'll explain in a moment. Quite powerful, in lambs zearalenone causes more rapid and greater weight gain than even *Saccharomyces cerevisiae*, or brewer's yeast.[16]

Hormones actually predate antibiotics in terms of their use as growth promoters. As early as the 1930s, farmers injected cows with an extract of bovine pituitary hormone to induce the animals to produce more milk.[17] Bovine somatotropin was later identified as the chemical component responsible for this action. The FDA approved a recombinant form of the hormone in 1993. Recombinant bovine growth hormone (rbGH) is also known as recombinant bovine somatotropin (rbST). Today, as many as a third of dairy cattle are still given rbST, despite a continuing surplus of milk.[18]

The use of some hormones has been documented as a health risk. Also in the 1930s, scientists succeeded in isolating various forms of estrogen. Cattle and poultry injected with the female growth hormone gained weight more quickly. By the 1950s, diethylstilbestrol (DES) had become the most popular form of estrogen added to livestock feed. When its connection with human cervical cancer and birth defects was discovered in the 1970s, DES was removed from the market.[19]

> "McDonald's wants suppliers of meat to limit antibiotic use
>
> The policy by the world's largest restaurant company aims to phase-out so-called growth-promotion antibiotics, which are also used in human medicine. In livestock, these antibiotics are laced into animal feed in low doses to make animals grow faster. McDonald's said meat suppliers have until the end of next year to comply.
>
> Roughly 20 million pounds of antibiotics are given each year to U.S. cattle, pigs, and chickens. Many of the drugs are administered routinely to healthy livestock solely as a preventive measure and *to promote growth*. Farmers can buy many livestock antibiotics without a prescription."[21]

Hormones, antibiotics fed to livestock — and thence to us

Without actually testing it, it is difficult to say whether the steak on your plate definitely contains a residue of the antibiotics and hormones fed to the cow from which it was taken. Remember, the reason the European Community cites for its ban on antibiotics for livestock is the worry that the practice could lead to the infection of human consumers by superstrains of resistant bacteria — not a fear that the meat from such animals contains an antibiotic residue. However, given events such as the estrogen scandal of the 1970s (referred to one paragraph above), we should do our best to avoid meat from antibiotic and hormone-fed livestock. It helps to know that here in the United States, hormones are fed only to cattle and sheep. They tend to cause poultry to gain too much fat, while pigs fail to respond to them very much at all.[20] So, the easiest way to avoid hormones is to restrict your meat consumption to pork, poultry and fish. On the other hand, not all poultry and pig farmers refrain from using antibiotics. So, when you buy any kind of meat, read the labels and try to find brands that are raised without the use of hormones and antibiotics. Incidentally, grass-fed livestock also count as the best source of protein.

The use of antibiotics and hormones by beef and chicken suppliers to fast food companies has come under increased scrutiny. Environmental and health-watch groups have succeeded in convincing McDonald's to phase out the use of meat from such suppliers *(see box on opposite page)*. Proactive moves by such industry leaders will help, but minimizing overall exposure to antibiotics remains the responsibility of every individual.

1. TLJ Lawrence, Growth of Farm Animals, 2nd ed. 2002.

2. Lawrence, TLJ, and Fowler, VR. Growth of Farm Animals, 2nd ed. CAB International. 2002. CABI-Publishing.org/bookshop/ReadingRoom/0851194849.asp. Pp 320-330-Chapter 15.

3. Ibid.

4. American Society for Microbiology Comments on the Preservation of Antibiotics for Human Treatment Act of 2002. June 19, 2002. www.asmusa.org/pasrc/browncom.htm).

5. Blackwell, T. Antimicrobial growth promoters: what good are they? Ontario Ministry of Agriculture and Food. www.gov.on.ca/OMAFRA/english/livestock/swine/facts/info_hh_antimicrobial.htm, May 2003; **ALSO** Wegener, H.C, et al. Use of antimicrobial growth promoters in food animals and enterococcus faecium resistance to therapeutic antimicrobial drugs in Europe. CDC. Emerging Infectious Diseases, Vol 5, No 3. www.cdc.gov/ncidod/EID/vol5no3/wegener.htm)

6. Lawrence, TL J, and Fowler, VR. Growth of Farm Animals, 2nd ed. CAB International. 2002. CABI-Publishing.org/bookshop/ReadingRoom/0851194849.asp. Pp 320-330-Chapter 15.

7. Ibid.

8. Scott, E., Powell, K. Acute Otits Media. Medscape.com. June 6, 2003.

9. Ibid.

10. Chapman, R. Candida infections in the neonate. Curr Opin Pediatr 2003 Feb;15(1):97-102.

11. Goldman, E. Rapid weight gain in infancy predicts obesity. Family Practice News Online. Jan 15, 2002. Vol 32, No. 2.

12. Baldwin, R. The Fungus Fighters: Two Women and their Discovery. Cornell University Press. 1981.

13. USP DI. United States Pharmacopeia Drug information for the health care professional. 23rd ed. Micromedex. 2003.

14. American Livestock Supply, Inc. Label info for Ralgro. www.americanlivestock.com/showLabelInfo.jsp?productFamilyId=998, May 2003.

15. CAST, 2003.

16. Jones, B.A., et al. Effect of zeranol implantation and yeast supplementation on performance and carcass traits of finishing Wether lambs. Sheep and Goat Research Journal. Vol. 13, No 1:1997. http://ag.ansc.purdue.edu/sheep/research/effectseranol.html.

17. Lawrence, TL J, and Fowler, VR. Growth of Farm Animals, 2nd ed. CAB International. 2002. CABI-Publishing.org/bookshop/ReadingRoom/0851194849.asp. Pp 320-330-Chapter 15.

18. Ledger, H. USDA to provide feed assistance to drought-stricken NE ranchers. The Ledger Online. June 2003. http://www.ledgeronline.com/cgi-bin/artman/exec/view.cgi?archive=6&num=834&printer=1.

19. Cornell Univesity Program on Breast Cancer and Environmental Risk Factors in New York State. Fact sheet #37. June 2000.

20. Society for Endocrinology. Topical Briefings: Growth promoting hormones in cattle-the scientific evidence. May 2003. www.endocrinology.org/sfe/cattle.htm.

21. Leung, S. McDonal's wants suppliers of meat to limit antibiotics use. The Wall Street Journal. Friday, June 20, 2003.

Chapter 4
The problem with standard dietary recommendations

In this chapter, we investigate the connection between dietary recommendations and obesity trends over the last 40 years. Along the way, we take a look at the difference between being overweight, as opposed to being clinically obese.

"Overweight" vs. "obese"

As mentioned earlier, close to two-thirds of Americans are now overweight or obese. Specifically, 35 percent are overweight, while 27 percent are obese. "Overweight" implies a body mass index of between 25 to 29. Obesity is defined by a BMI of 30 or higher, while a BMI of more than 40 indicates "extreme obesity." The last class has shown a disturbing rise for both adults and children in the past several years.[1]

A couple of examples are in order. Under BMI guidelines, a six-foot, two-inch tall man would be considered overweight as soon as the needle on his scale reached 194 pounds. Add another 39 pounds to bring him to 233, and he would be obese. A woman five feet, five inches in height would be overweight at 150 pounds, and obese at 180 pounds.

You can calculate your Body Mass Index (BMI) by dividing your weight in kilograms by the square of your height in meters. Or,

Body Mass Index[3]

		overweight		obese	

BMI→ (kg/m²)	19	20	21	22	23	24	25	26	27	28	29	30	35	40
Height (inches)						Weight in pounds								
58	91	96	100	105	110	115	119	124	129	134	138	143	167	191
59	94	99	104	109	114	119	124	128	133	138	143	148	173	198
60	97	102	107	112	118	123	128	133	138	143	148	153	179	204
61	100	106	111	116	122	127	132	137	143	148	153	158	185	211
62	104	109	115	120	126	131	136	142	147	153	158	164	191	218
63	107	113	118	124	130	135	141	146	152	158	163	169	197	225
64	110	116	122	128	134	140	145	151	157	163	169	174	204	232
65	114	120	126	132	138	144	150	156	162	168	174	180	210	240
66	118	124	128	136	142	148	155	161	167	173	179	186	216	247
67	121	127	132	140	146	153	159	166	172	178	185	191	223	255
68	125	131	136	144	151	158	164	171	177	184	190	197	230	262
69	128	135	142	149	155	162	169	176	182	189	196	203	236	270
70	132	139	146	153	160	167	174	181	188	195	202	207	243	278
71	136	143	150	157	165	172	179	186	193	200	208	215	250	286
72	140	147	154	162	169	177	184	191	199	206	213	221	258	294
73	144	151	159	166	174	182	189	197	204	212	219	227	265	302
74	148	155	163	171	179	186	194	202	210	218	225	233	272	311
75	152	160	168	176	184	192	200	208	216	224	232	240	279	319
76	156	164	172	180	189	197	205	213	221	230	238	246	287	328

take your weight in pounds, multiply by 705 and divide by your height, in inches, twice.[2]

BMI trends vs. dietary recommendations

By and large, studies show that obesity numbers began a sharp rise to their present levels right around 1980. Specifically, one American study documents a significant increase between 1978 and 1991. Another study cites a significant rise in adult obesity between 1988 and 1994, despite relatively stable numbers between 1960 and 1980.[4] Further studies in 1999 and 2000 document the trend that began 25 years ago as continuing today.[5]

It stands to reason that a change in something, likely a life-style factor, has caused the jump in numbers. To see what that might be, let's take a look at what the U.S. Department of Agriculture has recommended we eat over the years — both through dieticians, physicians and literature and through its control of influential institutions such as the public school lunch.

Between 1956 and 1979, the USDA went with its "Basic Four" food groups. The guide is in part defined by the absence of specific cautions against eating too many fats.[6]

From 1979 to 1984 — roughly about the time more and more Americans started to get heavier and heavier — the USDA switched to its "Hassle Free Daily Food Guide." This plan preceded the introduction of the "Food Pyramid" we are advised to follow today. Significantly, it includes the USDA's first warning against eating too much fat,[7] a caution that remains in place today.

The Center for Nutrition Policy and Promotion (CNPP) joins the USDA as another non-corporate entity that pushes grains and sugars. The CNPP collates and then applies available and relevant scientific research to developing its *Dietary Guidelines for Americans*. In addition to the biannual *Family Economics and Nutrition Review*, the organization's many publications include a pamphlet entitled *Get on the Grain Train*.[8] This pamphlet stresses the importance of following the USDA Food Pyramid.

Ultimately, warnings against eating too much fat may have only served to reinforce the recommendation that we get most of our calories from grains. In other words, carbohydrates have become the "safe" food both by default and by design. Low-fat versions of foods higher in sugar than a brand's standard line have hit supermarket shelves with a vengeance. Splurging on such foods has been assumed to be the healthier way to live. Unfortunately, we've overlooked that carbohydrates such as grains and certain fruits are commonly contaminated with mycotoxins.

Grains and important nutritional institutions' misguided advice concerning them are not our only problem. According to the USDA's Economic Research Service, the average American eats more than 150 pounds of sugar every year. Despite this, dieticians with the National Academy of Sciences' Food Nutrition Board maintain that getting up to 25 percent of our total calories from added sugars is okay.[9] Think about that. A major institution in nutrition says it's okay to have *added* sugars — not counting the sugars present in a lot of foods already — make up *one quarter* of the calories we eat.

The National Soft Drink Association takes up where the science academy leaves off. The association challenges evidence linking carbohydrates such as sugar to obesity and numerous, other health problems. In an article in the Center for Nutrition Policy and Promotion's *Family Economics and Nutrition Review*, the soft drink advocacy group states that "the intake of added sugars is not directly related to diabetes, heart disease, obesity, and hyperactivity as was previously thought."[10]

A 1997 Sugar Association study takes the pro-sugar argument to its logical extreme. The association found that you can lose weight on a high-sugar, low-fat diet just as easily as you can on a low-sugar, low-fat diet. Its study was published in the American Journal of Clinical Nutrition, which happens to be the dietician's *bible*. If publications such as the AJCN can print this kind of hogwash, what kind of information are dieticians giving out to their clients?

This advice has persisted throughout the years, even though our bodies are masters at converting excess carbohydrates to fat. An old, human physiological chemistry textbook attests to this fact. "That animals may be fattened on a predominantly carbohydrate diet," reads the text, "demonstrates the ease of conversion of carbohydrates into fat."[11]

Would grain and sugar interests go so far as to intentionally spin studies and stats in their favor? Probably. On the other hand, the soft drink group — and the USDA, for that matter — may actually be in the right about sugars and carbohydrates, at least on the point that sugar *by itself* does not cause disease. After all, according to the American Diabetes Association, a third of diabetics will *still* suffer organ damage even if they manage to keep their blood sugar levels under control. In other words, another factor *besides* sugar lies behind the complications of heart disease, blindness, nerve damage and kidney disease that every diabetic is in danger of developing. (for more on this, please call our office to order a copy of our book, Infectious Diabetes). We believe fungi and their mycotoxins to be that factor.

You see, sugar counts as fungi's fuel of choice. As mentioned earlier, as well, according to leading, agricultural experts, many of the grains the USDA encourages us to eat run a high risk of contamination by, once again, fungi and their mycotoxins. In other words, the only way the USDA's recommendations could be more pro-fungi would be to draw in pictures of the microbes next to the loaf of bread that appears in the base of the pyramid!

To wrap things up, let's look at some specifics of the Food Pyramid. The plan recommends that teenaged boys and active men eat 11 servings of grains per day, and that children eat at least 6 servings. One serving comes to a half cup of food. For example, one way to eat 11 servings of grains would be to include two slices of toast and a cup of cereal with breakfast, two cups of pasta and nine pretzels with lunch, a cup of rice and a bread roll with dinner, followed by three cups of popcorn as an evening snack.

Of course, add a couple of sodas to your 11 servings of carbohydrates, and you've easily exceeded not only the USDA's recommendations — quite likely you've also exceeded your body's energy requirements for the day, as well. On top of that, rather than exercise, follow a day at your sedentary job with the American average of four hours of television. Take the antibiotics your doctor prescribed for you that may or may not be necessary. Ultimately, you will have succeeded in mimicking the life-style of a farm animal. After all, to fatten their livestock, farmers feed them lots of grains and antibiotics, and they keep them locked up in stalls to prevent them from exercising.

1. Freedman, D. et al. Trends and correlates of class 3 obesity in the US from 1990 through 2000. JAMA. Oct 9,2002. Vol 288, no 14.

2. Blackburn, G., et al. The obesity epidemic: prevention and treatment of the metabolic syndrome. Sept 18, 2002, Medscape.com.

3. Based on the chart at http://www.consumer.gov/weightloss/bmi.htm.

4. Flegal, K., et al. Prevalence and trends in obesity among US adults, 1999-2000. JAMA. Oct 9,2002. Vol 288, no 14.

5. Ibid.

6. http://www.nal.usda.gov/fnic/history/. June 2003.

7. Ibid.

8. Publications and Reports. www.usda.gov/cnpp. June 2003.

9. Sawyer-Morse, M. Sweet news on sugar. Today's Dietician. March 2003, p. 50-55.

10. Press Release. Daily Physical education and a balanced diet are the keys to combating childhood obesity: New science shows soft drinks not the cause of obesity or other chronic diseases. The National Soft Drink Association. NSDA.org. June 2003.

11. Harper, H., et al. Review of Physiological Chemistry, 16th ed. Lange Medical Publications. California. 1977.

Kaufmann and Holland

Chapter 5
Food
Organic or Conventional?

It goes without saying that changing what you eat can have a greater impact upon your health than any other life-style change you can make. The real question for a lot of people is, to what degree do we need to alter our diets to get the results we want?

A number of issues lie within this question, including whether or not we should buy *organic*. Do the benefits such foods bring with them make them worth the higher price?

What is organic food?
Briefly, organic farming is the raising of livestock for the market without the use of laboratory-derived growth hormones or antibiotics. The system requires the use of grain feed that has been grown according to organic standards. Such grain has not been sprayed with pesticides or herbicides, nor has it been genetically modified, fertilized with petroleum-based chemicals, or sterilized with ionizing radiation.[1,2]

Besides the absence of any impurities from sprays and the like, organic foods have a number of things going for them. For one thing, the fish or manure-based fertilizers that organic grain farmers use can make chemical pesticides unnecessary — strong, healthy plants fertilized by rich, natural substances tend to be more resistant to insect and mold damage. Finally, farms that produce organic grains, meat and dairy products also use farming techniques that are environmentally friendly, especially when compared with techniques practiced by the large, corporate agribusinesses.

For a farm or processing facility to be able to use "organic" labels, its products must be certified by a U.S. Department of Agriculture (USDA) agency. Often, these agencies are private organizations who charge a hefty, annual sum in exchange for a onetime, informal inspection and set of "certified organic" labels. Products touting this label must contain at least 95 percent organic ingredients.

"Organic" not always "natural"

Although the organic label permits it, I should tell you that it is hardly "natural" for cattle to eat corn-based feed, whether they are "free-roaming" or confined to a stall. The natural and therefore ideal scenario would be for cattle to graze in open fields on a variety of grasses. Unfortunately, accreditation agencies empowered to hand out "natural" food labels have yet to be created. So, before you go one level beyond organic and spend the extra money to buy range-free, grass-fed beef, make sure you do your homework. For example, some farmers practice a technique called marbling, in which cattle that have been fed grass throughout their lives are fed massive amounts of corn in the last few weeks before they are taken to market. Given corn's extreme vulnerability to mycotoxin contamination, an investment in beef from cattle raised in this manner is quite possibly a waste of money.

Organic produce and fungal contamination

As mentioned earlier, the risks are high that fruits and grains will become contaminated by fungi and mycotoxins at some point during the growing season and harvest and storage processes. The danger is real that these contaminants will be passed on to the animals and humans who eat such grains. Now, it so happens that conventional farmers use fungicides in an effort to limit this risk. On the other hand, because the "organic" label prohibits the spraying of crops with pesticides and other chemicals, fungicides are also not permitted. This means that, compared to their conventional counterparts, some organic foods — mainly fruits and grains — can run a higher risk of becoming contaminated by fungi.

Certainly, crops fertilized with fish byproducts or manure — rather than the chemicals used in conventional farming — can often become more resistant to insect and mold infestation. But studies have proved that there is no guarantee that this will happen. In addition, a plant "resistant" on the vine thanks to organic growing techniques doesn't necessarily remain resistant once it is processed — when a plant or grain either becomes damaged or goes into storage, it runs a risk of fungal contamination regardless as to how it was raised.

Apples illustrate the problem that can happen with organic produce. The fruit is vulnerable to contamination by a mycotoxin called patulin. Patulin is produced by several of the *Aspergillus* molds and at least one of the *Penicillium* species. Livestock fed grain contaminated with the chemical may suffer from immune suppression, swelling of the brain or intestines, cancer and premature death.[6]

Although the FDA recommends that patulin levels remain below 50 micrograms per liter in processed apple products,[5] levels of the mycotoxin in conventionally produced apple juice fall between 244 and 3,993 mcg/l. It gets worse. Patulin levels in *organic* apple juice can approach a whopping 45,000 mcg/l.[4] Although both the conventional and organic versions exceed the FDA's recommended level by a wide margin, *organic* apple products are clearly the far more dangerous choice.

Despite this, some complementary and alternative medicine practitioners have their patients undergo intestinal and gall bladder flushes with large amounts of organic apple cider or apple juice. This practice could be dangerous in the long run. At the very least, conventional apple juice would be the safer choice.

On the other hand, sometimes the organic version of a food turns out to have a lower risk of fungal contamination. In another study, when genetically-modified corn was exposed to large numbers of insects, it became more susceptible to contamination by *Fusarium* molds than organic corn proved to be.[7] Of course, given corn's general vulnerability to contamination,[8] neither the organic nor the genetically-modified types offer benefits that outweigh their risks.

Intelligent shopping

Ultimately, whether it be organic or conventional, you should weigh a food's risk of fungal contamination against its antifungal possibilities when you go shopping. For example, most strong-colored vegetables that go into salads — despite high carbohydrate levels as with carrots — possess innate, antifungal properties. So, including these foods is a wise choice in any diet. Aside from carrots, broccoli and garlic also have innate, antifungal properties that protect them from fungi.

It's also a good idea to find out exactly how your brand of fish, beef or chicken was fed. Specifically, steaks from a free-range cow fed moldy organic grain the farmer scattered on the ground would offer very little advantage over those obtained from a cow confined to a stall and injected with hormones and antibiotics and forced to eat grains from a sterile bin. Conversely, corn-fed or farm-raised fish are not only potential reservoirs for mycotoxins. Such seafood also has nowhere near the levels of beneficial, omega fatty acids found in ocean-caught fish. The bottom line here is that you absolutely must carefully consider what to buy and what not to buy, and you must also always strive to continue your education regarding nutrition.

Doug and I generally take the stance that organic, unblemished, non-starchy vegetables and most, organically grown, fresh fruits (bananas excluded because of their high risk of *Fusarium* mold contamination), together with organically grown nuts and eggs are safer and healthier than their conventional counterparts. For example, we try to feed our children organic yogurt and prepare them salads made with organic vegetables. As for meats, milk, butter, yogurt, poultry and fish: grass fed livestock and wild fish are better for you than conventionally raised stock. Certainly, we'd much rather sizzle grass-fed steaks on our grills than those from a hormone-injected, antibiotic-fed cow.

When it comes to grains, because of the contamination risks, most people — especially if they are battling chronic disease — need to minimize their intake. If you must eat grains, however, oats, rice, and beans have historically proved less susceptible to fungal contamination.[10]

1. National Food Processors Association. Nfpa-food.org. 4/2003.

2. ams.usda.gov/nop/Consumers/brochure.html. 4/2003.

3. "Mycotoxins: Risks in Plant, Animal, and Human Systems." Council for Agricultural Science and Technology Task Force Report No. 139. Ames, Iowa. Jan 2003.

4. Lovejoy, S. "Are Organic Foods Safer??" Greensmiths.com/organicfoods.html.

5. CAST 2003.

6. Ibid.

7. Munkvold, G, et al. "Comparison of fumonisin concentrations in kernels of transgenic Bt maize hybrids and nontransgenic hybrids." Biotech-info.net/Fusarium_abstract.html. 2003.

8. CAST 2003.

9. Etzel, R. "Mycotoxins." JAMA. Vol 287, No 4. Jan 23/30. 2002.

10. CAST. Council for Agricultural Science and Technology. Mycotoxins: economic and health risks. Report No. 116. Nov. 1989. Ames, IA.

Chapter 6

Metabolic Syndrome and fatty liver disease

A frequent precursor and predictor of diabetes and heart disease, Metabolic Syndrome is sometimes called "Syndrome-X." It is diagnosed when three of the following five conditions are present: high triglycerides, low levels of good cholesterol, high blood pressure, high blood sugar and finally, abdominal obesity. About one in four Americans have Metabolic Syndrome, for a total of some 47 million. For what it's worth, thus far one in 16 of us has

---

Diagnosing Metabolic Syndrome[2]

Having three of the following indictates Metabolic Syndrome.

1. Abdominal obesity (waist circumference = more than 40 inches in men and 35 inches in women)

2. Hypertriglyceridemia (a triglyceride level of 150mg/dl or greater)

3. Low HDL cholesterol (less than 40mg/dl in men and 50mg/dl in women)

4. High blood pressure (130/85 or greater)

5. High fasting glucose (Impaired glucose tolerance, or IGT— a fasting blood sugar between 110 and 126mg/dl)

---

type 2 diabetes. Researchers predict that this number will rise dramatically in the next few years.

Pinpointing the cause of either Metabolic Syndrome or diabetes has proved difficult. In one study, 67 percent of subjects who had developed Metabolic Syndrome were not just overweight, but actually clinically obese. On the other hand, 18 percent of the individuals studied were of normal body weight,[1] Match this against American Diabetes Association stats that show 10 percent of type 2 diabetics also tend not to be overweight. Clearly, excess fat in and of itself guarantees neither problem. On the other hand, because a majority of people who suffer from either disease *are* overweight, it makes sense to say that something about the life-style that leads people to put on excess fat likely plays a role in their developing the disease. The question would then be, what life-style habits are practiced by both the obese and the normal-weight people who develop the syndrome?

Scientists believe that the answer to this question is "improper nutrition and inadequate physical activity."[3] Their theory is seemingly supported by the fact that every single symptom of the syndrome can be reversed by weight loss.[4]

Now, what is "improper" nutrition? With the obesity epidemic flourishing in the face of our government and medical society-based dietary guidelines, could the guidelines themselves be "improper?" I speak, of course, of the Food Pyramid.

I should tell you that recently, a statistic in defense of the Pyramid has been issued: researchers maintain that only about 3 percent of Americans follow it. If that is true, then it follows that it would be difficult to blame the Pyramid for anything at all, including the obesity epidemic.

On the other hand, the 3 percent stat could just be smoke and mirrors. In fact, the Pyramid does not have to be followed to the letter for its pro-carbohydrate, anti-fat impact to be felt. Remember the switch to baked corn chips and pretzels, to low-fat ice cream higher in sugar than a given brand's regular version, and to labels maintaining the healthiness of dozens of high-carbohydrate snacks because they happened to have "only one gram of fat?" This movement gets its backing from the Food Pyramid. Have Americans lose weight — or at least stop gaining weight — as a result? Clearly we have not.

Again, a high-carbohydrate, low-fat diet puts the weight on not just because carbohydrates are easily converted into body fat.[5] More importantly, the grains and sugars with which carbohydrate-based foods are made are contaminated by *mycotoxins*.[6] These mycotoxins impact our body chemistries in such a way that we become net fat producers, rather than fat burners. In conjunction with a fungal infection, they can make us crave sugars and starchy foods and elevate our blood pressure. The result — a vicious cycle of spiraling weight gain and a high risk of developing Metabolic Syndrome.

Non-alcohol related fatty liver disease & Metabolic Syndrome

Close to three quarters of patients with Metabolic Syndrome also have what's called *nonalcoholic steatohepatitis* (NASH). Similar to what can happen in the livers of alcoholics who fail to control their drinking, the condition describes a liver weakened by inflammation and riddled with fatty deposits. Over time, NASH leads to cirrhosis — irreversible scarring much like that seen in kidney failure — in a quarter of all cases. Close to one in seven NASH cases end in death, usually due to liver failure.[7] Incidentally, in a study presented to the Pediatric Academic Societies meeting (Seattle, May 2003), 13 percent of the obese toddlers who participated tested positive for abnormal liver function.[8]

In the same way that large percentages of people with diabetes and hypertension will eventually develop kidney failure and require dialysis, doctors worry that the millions of Americans with metabolic syndrome will develop NASH and end up needing liver transplants.[9] This has raised the stakes for finding a cause and then a cure.

Although scientists suspect that insulin resistance plays a contributing role in the development of NASH, most remain in the dark as to what really causes the disease.[10] We would argue to you that the same thing that causes Metabolic Syndrome also causes NASH — mycotoxins. For example, aflatoxin is produced by the fungus, *Aspergillus*. This particular mycotoxin has been shown to cause fatty liver, hepatitis (inflammation of the liver) and fibrosis (scarring) in both humans and animals.[11] *Aspergillus* (and *Penicillium* as well) also produces a mycotoxin called ochratoxin. This second toxin has been linked to fatty liver in humans and animals.[12] Scientists may in fact be right in their suspicions of insulin resistance as a precursor to NASH. In any case, mycotoxins such as streptozotocin have in turn been demonstrated as capable of causing insulin resistance[13] — one of the defining characteristics of both Metabolic Syndrome and type 2 diabetes.

Interestingly, tissue work-ups of livers damaged by fatty deposits not connected with alcohol abuse appear "almost identical" to those taken from the damaged livers of alcoholics.[14] Remember, alcohol is a mycotoxin produced by brewer's yeast (*Saccharomyces cerevisiae*). It only makes sense that damage caused by alcohol would resemble the liver damage we suspect as being caused by other mycotoxins.

To sum up, we have a population of people eating high-carbohydrate, low-fat diets thanks largely to the influence of the grain-based Food Pyramid. These same people are also likely being prescribed unnecessary antibiotics by their doctors at previously unheard of rates. It should come as no surprise that such a group would develop the classic symptoms of mycotoxin exposure, otherwise known as conditions such as Metabolic Syndrome and NASH.

1. Marchesini, G., et al. Nonalcoholic fatty liver, steatohepatitis, and the metabolic syndrome. Hepatology 2003 April;37(4):917-23).

2. Blackburn, G, et al. The Obesity Epidemic: Prevention and Treatment of the Metabolic Syndrome. Medscape.com. Released Sept 18, 2002.

3. Ibid.

4. Ibid.

5. Harper, et al. Review of Physiological Chemistry, 16th ed. Los Altos, California. 1977.

6. Etzel, R. Mycotoxins. *Journal of the American Medical Association.* 287(4). Jan 23/30, 2002.

7. Resnick, R., Chopra, S. Nonalcoholoic steatohepatits: A common hepatic disorder. Family Practice Recertification. Vol 24, No. 9. Aug 2002.

8. Mercola, J. Why are so many toddlers obese? Mercola.com, May 2003.

9. Marchesini, G., et al. Nonalcoholic fatty liver, steatohepatitis, and the metabolic syndrome. Hepatology 2003 April;37(4):917-23.

10. Russo, M; Jacobson, I. Nonalcoholic fatty liver disease. Hospital Physician, Nov 2002.

11. CAST. Mycotoxins: Risks in plant, animal, and human systems. Task force report No 139, Jan 2003. Council for Agricultural Science and Technology, Ames, IA).

12. Class course in Advanced Food Microbiology. Microbial foodborne pathogens. http://class.fst.ohio-state.edu/fst736/sect4.htm. June 2003.

13. ID TNO Animal Nutrition. Diabetic pig characterized by hepatic and cellular insulin-resistance. http://www.id.dlo.nl/ID-Lelystad/documenten/flyers/IDTNO 22.0701_koopmans_uk.pdf).

14. Kichian, K., et al. Nonalcoholic fatty liver disease in patients investigated for elevated liver enzymes. Canadian Journal of Gastroenterology. 2003 Jan;17(1):38-42.

Part Two
Life-style Change

• •

Chapter 7
Testimonies
Weight Loss with Doug and Dr. Dave

Phyllis

Between croup, bronchitis and whooping cough, I spent a lot of time on antibiotics as a child. I wasn't constantly sick, but when it hit, it hit hard. Then around the age of nine, I started to feel as though I could never get enough to eat. I lived for eating all the goodies I could get my hands on. I often scoured our kitchen for food, my cravings were so intense. Soon, I began to put on excess weight.

As a teenager, like a lot of kids I ate mostly carbohydrates: pizza, hamburgers, sodas and ice cream. But although my friends ate normal amounts, I was driven to stuff myself and then go looking for more. I was pretty active — I went to a lot of dances and such — but I still continued to gain weight.

As an adult, I did my best to hide my addiction. I stashed bags of candy and cookies all over our house. I even hid ice cream in the freezer, so well that my husband Bill never knew it was there. Of course, the ice cream never stayed there for long. Most days, I planned what I would eat and how many drive-through restaurants I could visit. I knew where all the dumpsters were in town, so that I could quickly get rid of the evidence of my splurges. When sudden cravings hit me while we were out, I hid in the bathroom of wherever we happened to be at the time and ate one of the candy bars I'd stuffed into the bottom of my purse.

Eventually, I had to stop most of my activities because I either lacked the energy and stamina to do them, or my size made them impossible. My husband Bill had to go into a restaurant first to check it out and see if they had tables — booths were completely out of the question. I couldn't go to a movie —in fact, any place where the chairs had arms was off-limits. To shop at Wal-Mart, I had to use one of the motorized carts they keep on hand.

Bill tried to help. He joined me on a number of programs, including vegetarian diets and juice fasting. But we never stayed with anything for very long. By the year 2002, at the age of 52, I had reached my highest recorded weight — 400.2 pounds.

One day at rehearsal — we serve as worship leaders at our church — things went from bad to worse. When someone switched on the air conditioning, mold spores blew from the vent right into my face. We investigated, and we discovered that the basement that housed the air-conditioning unit was flooded — the walls were black with mold. Soon thereafter, I came down with a severe respiratory infection. I felt like I had bronchitis, asthma and pneumonia all at the same time. My lungs filled with fluid, and I could barely breathe. I felt I was going to literally cough myself to death. Lying in bed was impossible, so I had to sit in my recliner and lean forward with a pillow on a TV tray.

Out of desperation, I went to a walk-in clinic. The antibiotics I was given not only didn't seem to help, they made things worse. In the middle of the night, my heart sometimes pounded so hard that I woke up, positive I was about to have a heart attack. And even with all these problems, I still couldn't make myself stop eating.

Then one day, I happened to tune my television into the show, 'Your Health with Doug Kaufmann.' Doug spoke about fungus and how it can cause various diseases. By the time the show ended, I was on the phone ordering Doug's book, The Fungus Link.

Since Bill and I often read aloud to each other, I asked him to read it with me when it arrived, and he agreed. We were amazed at what we learned. In all our years of reading nutrition books, we had never learned anything quite like this.

At the end of the book, there was a diet to kill off the fungus and restore health. I asked Bill if he would go on the diet with me for support. He said yes, he would do anything to help me get healthy. January 28, 2002, we began the program and within weeks, my health began to improve. My lungs cleared up and I gained more energy. My acid reflux and indigestion literally vanished, my cracked heels and athlete's foot cleared up, and, of course, the weight began to come off.

When I had lost 33 pounds, I began an exercise program at a health spa. As of May, 2003, I have lost 160 pounds, and I have energy like I haven't had for years. I work out 3-5 times a week, walking fast and lifting weights. My heart feels strong, I'm more mentally alert and the excitement and joy I feel overwhelms me sometimes. Bill is thrilled. He's gotten his wife back, plus his health has improved, as well. He lost 20 pounds and has more energy. He now eats according to Doug's recommendations for his own health, and not just to get me to do it. We plan to continue eating healthy for the rest of our lives.

So, thank you so much Doug, Dr. Dave, Sherman, Mike, Bill, Ken and Gloria for helping me live. I still have close to 100 pounds to lose, but I know I'll make it and I will live happily and healthily ever after.

-Phyllis

Francie W.

I teach school in Jonesboro, Arkansas. Although I'm only 52, I've had some major health problems for several years. I am not only overweight — I have suffered from irritable bowel syndrome (IBS), arthritis, overactive bladder and, according to a doctor's October, 2002 diagnosis, I have also had lupus. Finally, by the time I started watching Doug Kaufmann's show, I'd also started having severe yeast break-outs. My doctor had me on anti-inflammatories and a number of other medications.

I bought Doug's book, The Fungus Link. Since then, I have followed his Intial Phase Diet for 2 weeks. Not only have I lost nine pounds — I no longer need to take any of the medications my doctor had me on. Instead, I am on a good vitamin and mineral regimen combined with Noni juice [*Noni* is a powerful antifugal].

I cannot say enough about Doug and his wonderful work, advise, and compassion. I wish I had listened long before now. I pray other people will listen. I pray that I will continue to improve. Thanks for listening and thank you Doug Kaufmann.

-Francie W.

Rich

I have been on the diet since July and have lost 33 pounds. I've never tried to lose weight before and I can hardly believe how the weight just came off without starving myself. My wife has been involved with support groups for weight loss but has thrown away her dieting books. She has lost 50+ pounds.

Blessed to be a blessing,

-Rich

Brenda M.

I have been watching Doug's show for about a year now. The information that he has presented has been a lifesaver for me. Since last October, I have been on the Initial Phase and InterPhase diets. As a result, I have gotten off all my prescriptions for asthma, high blood pressure, high cholesterol and GERD [all conditions addressed in The Fungus Link]. And I've lost 20 pounds. I have also been on a rotation of the antifungals Doug recommends, and now I take probiotics everyday. I tell everyone I can about the show and what Doug is talking about.

God bless you all, and keep up the good work!!

-Brenda M.

Dan

My wife Carolyn and I attend the same church as Dr. Dave and his family. Carolyn happened to hear about the doctor's work one day. She began the diet program that he recommends around Easter of 2003. Her health quickly improved a great deal, and she lost a substantial amount of weight. She encouraged me to read The Fungus Link [Dr. Holland is co-author] and consider going on the diet myself.

I hesitated. I'd never more than glanced at any of the diet plans publishers seem to keep coming out with, but I *had* watched friends lose a lot of weight only to gain all of it back, and more. On the other hand, I'd seen my wife get results. And, unlike the plans my friends have tried, she'd continued to eat pretty much like a normal person without "starving" herself. Of course, when she told me I would have to give up Cokes, I thought, "This is impossible, I can never succeed at this." But, at 52 years old, 5 feet, 10 inches and 260 pounds, I figured it was time I made a change.

I began the Initial Phase diet in May, switching to InterPhase two weeks later. I always had plenty to eat, but remarkably enough, I lost weight quickly. By August, I had lost about 55 pounds.

Many thanks and a tip of the hat to Dr. Dave.
-Dan

Wife's post-script:

Dan's house-shaking snore has dropped to a purr, and his chronic cough has gotten much better. He also has fewer headaches and has been able to stop popping antacids and antihistamines. Perhaps most importantly, he has much more energy to help out around the house!

Chapter 8
The Kaufmann Antifungal Program

Section 1: An Overview

A recent study in the American Journal of Preventive Medicine concludes that poor diet and its links to obesity, diabetes, heart disease and cancer cause up to a million deaths a year in the United States alone.[1] Despite this, most physicians make a point of discussing nutrition in only about a quarter of their consultations. Even when they do take the time to give advice on eating habits, they spend an average of less than a minute on the subject with each of their patients. Add to this the fact that most of the nutritional "experts" involved in training physicians teach that the sole problem with sugar is that it causes cavities, and you have one, bleak picture.

We believe that sound, nutritional advice that includes a strategy to fight fungi and prevent them from causing disease is *crucial* to maximizing good health.

We've mentioned that mycology (study of fungi) experts have understood the importance of low-carb diets in combatting fungi since as early as 1944.[2] The evidence linking fungi and diseases such as diabetes and heart disease that we have laid out in this book — reinforced by the success we experienced treating patients at our former clinic — has convinced us that the same, low-carbohydrate diet can both cure such diseases and even prevent them from developing in the first place.

The low-carbohydrate component works because it starves fungi of the sugar they need to live and grow. Cutting carbs is only one part of the strategy, however. Otherwise, we would recommend that you simply get on a program such as the *Atkins Diet*, or A. Scott Connelly's *Body RX*. As it turns out, to further improve health and drop the risks of developing diabetes and heart disease, we have found that cutting foods commonly contaminated by fungi and their mycotoxins is also necessary. Finally, we have added a third component — increasing foods rich in natural antifungals.

In addition to the Initial Phase Diet, you should also consider taking antifungal supplements or medications in order to more effectively decrease the active population of fungi in your intestines and throughout the rest of your body. If you are seriously ill or hospitalized with a stubborn or life-threatening fungal infection, you will likely need to take one of a number of very strong, prescription antifungals. Only a doctor can prescribe such medications. For milder cases, a number of potent, natural antifungals are available without a prescription in most health food stores.

Fiber in the form of psyllium hulls, together with replacement of the intestines' "good" bacteria, represents the final component of our antifungal program. Psyllium hulls — and a number of vegetables — help neutralize and eliminate the mycotoxins that contaminate the food we eat. They also help restore proper bowel function, essential to restoring and maintaining good health. In addition, replacement of beneficial, intestinal bacteria such as *L. acidophilus* killed off by the overuse of antibiotics, steroids, and immune-suppressing drugs can often cure constipation, bloating, gas, diarrhea, asthma and some allergies. Moreover, these bacteria produce chemicals that discourage fungal growth in the intestines.

The Antifungal Program in a Nutshell

1. Begin the Initial Phase Diet, a regimen low in carbohydrates that cuts simple sugars, yeast products and other foods commonly contaminated with fungi and their mycotoxins, and increases consumption of foods rich in antifungal nutrients.

2. Kill the fungi already in your body, with either prescriptive or natural antifungals.

3. Take psyllium hulls to both neutralize the mycotoxins in your body and to achieve and maintain regularity.

4. To discourage future growth of fungi and to improve bowel function, replace the good bacteria in your intestines that have been killed off by antibiotics and immunosuppressants.

5. Supplement with specific herbs, vitamins, or minerals that have been found to be useful in fighting a specific disease or symptom (i.e. chromium picolinate for obesity).

Taking supplements to replace a broad range of nutrients often lacking in our day-to-day diets makes sense. But, when starting the Initial Phase Diet (IPD), most people may want to stop all except the most essential supplements for the first couple of weeks, especially if the supplements you've been taking haven't been working against the illness you are fighting. After two weeks, it's usually okay to resume or begin taking a good, comprehensive multi-supplement. If you are pregnant or have specific concerns regarding various supplements, please consult with your doctor.

Section 2: Details of the Antifungal Program

1. Starve the fungi with the Initial Phase, InterPhase and Life Phase Diets.

Over the years, a number of studies have come together to prove that sugar is fungi's food of preference. In one such study, mice were fed straight table sugar. The ease and speed with which fungi in the mice's intestines grew and multiplied when exposed to large amounts of the fuel astonished scientists. Mice whose immune systems had been compromised by drugs or illness proved especially vulnerable to infection by the sugar-craving microbes.

Although fungal infections in the intestines can wreak a great deal of havoc, from there it gets even more serious. In the case of the mice, once they'd taken control in the mice's digestive tracts, the invaders penetrated the rodents' bloodstreams and spread throughout the rest of their bodies.[3]

Sugar belongs to the family of carbohydrates. "Carbohydrate" describes both the one-molecule forms such as the simple sugar, glucose, found in our bloodstreams, and complex, multimolecular polysaccharides such as starch. Although fungi can't process complex carbohydrates, because our bodies break down even the most complex of these into simple sugar for absorption into our bloodstreams, the invading microbes can eventually make a nice meal of anything from rye bread to linguini to french fries.

Fortunately, the fuel fungi crave can be used against them. They can literally be starved out by a diet low in carbohydrates. The upshot is, diet is by far the most important component of the Antifungal Program. In fact, until you remove sugar from your diet insofar as is possible, no amount of antifungal medications or supplements are likely to deliver adequate, long-term results.

Beyond denying food to the fungi that have already succeeded in infecting us, it is also important that we minimize our exposure to fungi and their mycotoxins in the future. Although both regularly contaminate grains and nuts to varying degrees, the USDA screens for no fungi and only one of mycotoxins that are known to cause disease — aflatoxin. This means that we have to play the odds in order to cut down on the amount of mycotoxins that ends up on our tables. In other words, random tests put forward by research groups such as CAST (Council for Agricultural Science and Technology) tell us exactly which foods carry high risks for contamination. So, although we can't simply point to and say with certainty that a given sample of grain or nuts has been compromised, we can make intelligent decisions about what we should eat, thereby drastically reducing our exposure. By way of example, random testing results tell us that when we avoid eating corn, peanuts and anything that contains them, we remove a major, potential source of mycotoxins from our diets.

By the same token, all three stages of diet in the antifungal plan also push certain vegetables that contain antifungal nutrients. As it turns out, vegetables such as garlic, carrots and broccoli are more than just antifungals. They have also been proven to neutralize the mycotoxins that fungi produce.

Initial Phase*
In most cases, we advise beginning with the Initial Phase diet, the toughest and most restrictive of our three regimens. The length of

*formerly known as the *Phase One* Diet

time you spend on it depends upon how quickly your condition improves, and how long you've had your symptoms. We've seen Initial Phase work in as quickly as two weeks, but the diet has sometimes required as long as a year. Everyone responds differently. In addition, you may need to return to Initial Phase from time to time, if your symptoms return or if you develop another fungal disease.

Feeling ill within a few days of starting the antifungal plan is not at all uncommon. This response is known as a Herxheimer's reaction, after Jarisch-Herxheimer.[4] It may leave you with flu-like symptoms or cause you to develop a skin rash. Although scientists do not fully understand the exact mechanism behind Herxheimer's, the evidence indicates that, when fungi experience extreme stress such as that caused by sugar deprivation, they spit out even more mycotoxins. The excess poison is one reason you may feel under the weather. In addition, as the fungi actually die, they release endotoxin-like substances and various antigens, which add to their soon-to-be ex-hosts' discomfort. Ironically enough, this "feeling terrible" is a clear sign that you are on the right track to healing yourself.[4] When you feel better, and as soon as your blood sugar levels stabilize — or your blood pressure drops down to acceptable levels — more than likely it's time to move from the Initial Phase Diet to the InterPhase Diet.

InterPhase*

Pregnant or nursing mothers and children should follow the Initial Phase Diet only under the strict supervision of a personal physician. InterPhase, with fewer restrictions than Initial Phase, is often a more appropriate program in such cases. Elite athletes may also

*formerly known as the *Phase Two* Diet

want to skip Initial Phase and start with InterPhase, because it allows consumption of more carbohydrates.

Among other things, the InterPhase diet recommends carbohydrates such as oats, rice, and beans, all of which run lower risks of fungal contamination than grains such as corn and wheat. You may stay on InterPhase for as long as you like. And, should you feel the need, the diet allows you the freedom to eat foods not specifically mentioned. Keep in mind, however, that if your symptoms return after you eat a particular food — say, popcorn or ham on rye, you will probably want to avoid that particular food insofar as is possible. Again, if you get sick again while you are on InterPhase, you may need to return to Initial Phase until your situation stabilizes once more.

2. Kill the fungi.

Two, broad groups of antifungals are available — natural and prescription. Only a doctor can prescribe pharmaceutical antifungals such as Diflucan (fluconazole), nystatin, Sporanox (itraconazole), Lamisil (terbinafine), and Nizoral (ketoconazole). In addition, hospitals use intravenous antifungals such as Amphotericin B and Cancidis to treat life-threatening, fungal infections.

Oral nystatin is an intestinal antifungal with no significant drug interactions or toxicity with regular use. The other, prescription medicines listed above are used to treat systemic fungal infections — those that have infested body tissues or fluids. Systemic antifungals are potentially more toxic. They also can even eventually damage the liver. Finally, combining systemic antifungals with other drugs can lead to harmful side-effects. This is especially true of the cholesterol-lowering and diabetic meds you may be taking. Your doctor and pharmacist will be able to give you more specific information on how to use such drugs safely and effectively.

In the long run, however, for life-threatening conditions such as diabetes and heart disease, the benefits of systemic antifungals likely outweigh the risks. So, under the supervision of your doctor, you might try combining a potent, systemic antifungal with a dose of nystatin for at least two weeks, to start with. Such a combination would go a long way toward effectively purging all of your bodily systems of fungi.

If you are unable to obtain prescription medicines, or would simply prefer not to take them, remember that a wide variety of powerful, natural antifungals lies at your disposal. In fact, without the naturally occurring chemicals that kill fungi, fungal growth would run amok.

Natural Antifungals

1. Olive Leaf Extract (OLE). Independent labs have demonstrated OLE's ability to eradicate disease-causing fungi. OLE contains oleuropein and other, active phytochemicals that act against the microbes.

2. Caprylic acid is a fatty acid derived from coconut oil. It has potent antifungal properties and usually comes in capsule form.

3. Pau d'arco comes packaged as a tea, or in capsule form. The substance is derived from the bark of the pau d'arco tree, which contains an assortment of fungicides. It's worth noting that, despite the high humidity of the rain forests where it is found, the pau d'arco tree does not grow mold or mildew on its bark.

4. Undecalynic acid, derived from the oil of caster beans, is an old, familiar antifungal used medicinally years before pharmaceutical antifungals came out. Several companies offer undecalynic acid in capsule form.

5. Malic acid derived from apple cider vinegar is an effective antifungal. Try diluting it with water or mixing it with fresh-squeezed carrot juice.

6. Garlic is perhaps the most well well-known, antifungal food worldwide. One of the phytoenzymes in garlic, allicin, has been documented to work against other microbes in addition to fungi. Many companies sell garlic as a supplement, but since allicin is best used synergistically with other enzymes contained in whole garlic, it is best (and most cost-efficient) to squeeze or grind a clove of the stuff into a glass of fresh carrot juice. If your family or office staff begins avoiding you, either reduce the amount of garlic you are taking or try a capsule form of garlic.

7. Carrots were the focus of a 1988 study in the Journal of Microbiology. Researchers maintained that the vegetables are excellent fungus fighters. On the downside, some scientists worry that carrots and carrot juice contain an excessive amount of carbohydrates. However, the antimicrobial, nutritional and enzymatic properties carrots have to offer far outweigh this drawback. In fact, a fresh-squeezed carrot juice in the morning with breakfast is the perfect way to start a day on — or off — the Initial Phase Diet. A decent juicer can run from $80-200. "Juice bars" are quite common now, as well, so it's easy to grab a carrot juice, even on the run.

8. Tea tree oil is an effective topical antifungal available in health food stores. It is useful in treating skin or nail fungal infections.

A number of relatively recent papers highlight some exciting, antifungal remedies that have been studied for their effectiveness in preventing and treating a number of diseases, including cancer.

Among these number grapefruit seed extract (GSE), conjugated linoleic acids (CLA), oil of oregano, and the monoterpenes d-limonene (orange oil) and perillyl alcohol (Oil of Lavender). D-limonene is found in the essential oil of lemons, oranges, grapefruit, caraway, dill, bergamot, peppermint, spearmint, grasses and tomatoes. Oil of lavender, or perillyl alcohol, is distilled from lavender and may also be found in cherries, mint and celery seeds.

GSE has been found to be more effective at killing yeast than bleach, colloidal silver, tea tree oil, and iodine.[4] Oil of oregano is also a potent antifungal. Both of these products are available over-the-counter and have virtually no side effects, unless you count the bitter face you'll likely make when you taste them! GSE should be diluted with water, as spelled out in the directions on the label.

Conjugated linoleic acids are natural components of dairy, beef and lamb products. CLAs possess an impressive range of promising health benefits.[5] Not only have studies shown that they suppress cancer,[6] CLAs have also demonstrated the ability to enhance our immune systems, while protecting against the catabolic, or wasting away, effects of immune stimulation.[7] The benefits CLAs provide us toward other diseases such as diabetes and heart disease definitely deserve further study. It's worth noting that grass-fed beef has notably higher concentrations of CLAs than its grain-fed counterpart. Many small-time ranchers offer grass-fed beef products. Instead of grains stored for lengthy periods of time that in turn run a much higher risk of mycotoxin contamination, free-range cattle eat fresh grass that grows out on the open plain.

3. Get and keep those bowels moving.

It is imperative that, as you kill fungi, you make sure they are properly expelled from your body. This is a function of the bowels, and it is all too often a job poorly done. Even if your bowels are functioning normally, we recommend that you supplement with non-digestible fiber such as psyllium hulls or slippery elm. We say this because research has shown that psyllium hulls can bind mycotoxins in the intestines and carry them out of the body.[5] The powdered form of psyllium hulls works the best, and it can be found at most health food stores. Be sure to read the label. Some brands of powdered fiber contain sugar or artificial sweeteners that you should avoid while on the Initial Phase Diet. Powdered psyllium hulls may be taken just before bed (one tablespoon mixed with water) or throughout the day (one heaping teaspoon in water, twice daily). Be sure to drink plenty of water when taking these products, preferably of the bottled, spring, or reverse osmosis types.

If you are constipated and fiber fails to increase your regularity, you might try casgara sagrada. Casgara sagrada, found in health food stores, stimulates the peristalsis (involuntary movement of the intestines) but should not be taken for long periods of time. Once your situation improves, return to taking psyllium only.

Remember, please consult with your physician before taking regularity-related products if you have experienced blockage of the intestines in the past, or if you have had bowel surgery. In addition, if you suffer from severe constipation or rapid changes in bowel habits, you may also wish to ask your doctor whether diabetes, magnesium deficiency, thyroid disease or colon cancer might lie behind your condition. If you have inflammatory bowel disease (Crohn's disease or Ulcerative Colitis) or irritable bowel syndrome, you could benefit from our Antifungal Program. We offer more specific information on how to treat such diseases in one of our earlier books, The Fungus Link, available through our website, www.knowthecause.com.

4. Replace the good bacteria in your intestines, and minimize taking antibiotics and immunosuppressants in the future.

Repeated courses of antibiotics can cause "dysbiosis," or an altered bowel terrain. This can in turn give fungi a foothold in the intestines, or encourage their overgrowth if they have already established a foothold. If this has happened to you, gas, bloating, belching, constipation, diarrhea and cramps likely followed them. If this describes you to a T, after following the Initial Phase Diet for a couple of weeks, it might be wise to restore the normal flora of your intestines by taking a good, probiotic supplement. If you have severe symptoms, simply replenishing intestinal bacteria may not be enough. If fungi have had a chance to flourish, you may have to knock them out with a prescription, intestinal antifungal such as nystatin before replacing the protective bacteria (see step #3 above).

5. Supplement with specific herbs, vitamins, minerals — and an exercise program — that have been found to be useful in treating the disease you are targeting (see page 89).

1. HealthScoutNews. Docs Often Overlook Nutrition Counseling. Sept. 25, 2002.

2. Conant, N., et al. Manual of Clinical Mycology. 1944. W. B. Saunders Company. Philadelphia.1. Vargus, S.L., et al. Modulating effect of dietary carbohydrate supplementation on Candida albicans colonization and invasion in a neutropenic mouse model. Infection and immunity. 1993;61:619-626.

3. Dorland's Illustrated Medical Dictionary, 29th ed. Philadelphia: W.B. Saunders Co. 1994.

4. Costantini, M.D., et al. Fungalbionics Series: The Garden of Eden Longevity Diet- Antifungal-antimycotoxin diet for the prevention and treatment of cancer, atherosclerosis, and other degenerative diseases. Freiburg, Germany. 1998.

5. GSE Report, Volume 1, Issue 1, p.6. (Studies performed by Dr. John Mainarich of Bio-Research Laboratories in Redmond, WA).

5. McGuire, M.K.; McGuire, M.A.; Ritzenthaler, K.; Shultz, T.D. Dietary sources and intake of conjugated linoleic acid intake in humans. 1999. 369-377. In Yurawecz, M.P; Mossaoba, M.M.; Kramer, J.K.G.; Pariza, M.; Nelson, G.J. Advances in Conjugated Linoleic Acid Research. Volume 1. AOCS Press. Champaign, IL.

6. Parodi, P.W. Conjugated linoleic acid: the early years. 1999; 1-11. In Yurawecz M.P; Mossaoba, M.M.; Kramer, J.K.G.; Pariza, M.; Nelson, G.J. Advances in Conjugated Linoleic Acid Research. Volume 1. AOCS Press. Chanmpaign, IL.

7. Pariza, M. The biological activities of conjugated linoleic acid. 1999; 12-20. In Yurawecz, M.P; Mossaoba, M.M.; Kramer, J.K.G.; Pariza, M.; Nelson, G.J. Advances in Conjugated Linoleic Acid Research. Volume 1. AOCS Press. Champaign, IL.

I. The Initial Phase Diet

(formerly the Phase One Diet)

Food Groups	Foods ALLOWED on the diet	Foods EXCLUDED from the diet
1. Sugar	None[a]	All sugars excluded
2. Artificial and herbal sweeteners	Stevia, Stevia Plus	Aspartame, saccharin
3. Fruit	Green apples, berries, avocados, grapefruit, lemons, limes and fresh coconut	All others, including fruit juices
4. Meat	Virtually all meats, including fish, poultry and beef[b]	Breaded meats
5. Eggs	Yes, all types allowed	Avoid egg substitutes
6. Dairy[c]	Butter and yogurt (organic is best); sparingly: cream cheese, organic, unsweetened whipping cream, and real, sour cream	All others, including margarine and any of the butter substitutes
7. Vegetables	Most fresh, unblemished vegetables and freshly made vegetable juice[d]	Potatoes and legumes (beans and peas)
8. Beverages	Bottled or filtered water; non-fruity, herb teas; Stevia-sweetened, fresh lemonade or lime-ade	Coffee and tea (including decaf) and regular/diet sodas
9. Grains	Zero grains allowed	Pasta, rice, corn, wheat, quinoa, amaranth, millet, buckwheat, oats and barley
10. Yeast products	No yeast allowed	All are all *excluded*, as are bread, mushrooms, pastries and alcohol
11. Vinegars	Unpasteurized, apple cider vinegar and black olives not aged in vinegar	Pickles, salad dressings[e] green olives, soy sauce
12. Oils	Olive, grape or flax seed, and virgin coconut (cold-pressed is best)	Partially-hydrogenated ("trans") oils, corn and peanut oil
13. Nuts	Raw nuts, including pecans, almonds, walnuts, cashews, pumpkin seeds	Peanuts (and all peanut products) and pistachios are excluded.

(p. 84)

II. InterPhase

(formerly the Phase Two Diet)

Food Groups	Foods ALLOWED in the diet	Foods EXCLUDED from the diet
1. Sugar		
2. Artificial and herbal sweeteners	*Same as Initial Phase Diet for food groups number one through six.*	
3. Fruit		
4. Meat		
5. Eggs		
6. Dairy[c]		
7. Vegetables	Fresh, unblemished vegetables and freshly made vegetable juice,[d] *yams, legumes (beans and peas)*	Potatoes
8. Beverages	Bottled/filtered water; non-fruity, herb teas; Stevia-sweetened, fresh lemonade or lime-ade	Coffee and tea (including decaf) and sodas (diet sodas also excluded)
9. Grains	*Oats (oatmeal), brown rice, quinoa, amaranth, millet, buckwheat, barley, flour tortillas, sourdough bread* (in moderation)	Corn and yeast breads
10. Yeast Products		
11. Vinegars	*Same as Initial Phase Diet for food groups number ten through thirteen.*	
12. Oils		
13. Nuts		

Notes for Initial Phase and InterPhase

a. Honey may be used sparingly as a sweetner if needed.

b. Farm-raised meat and fish are corn-fed, so they should be kept to a minimum. Grass-fed beef is ideal, followed by organic meats to which antibiotic exposure has been minimized.

c. Dairy products are better if from range-fed cattle and animals not injected with antibiotics, hormones or steroids, nor fed with silo-stored grains. Good products include Brown Cow, Monarch Hills and Redwood Hills. Whipping cream is liquid, unsweetened, heavy cream.

d. Organically grown vegetables are preferred.

e. Excluded because many of them are fermented products.

III. LifePhase for Weight Maintenance

Food Groups	Foods that are ENCOURAGED	Foods that are DISCOURAGED
1. Sugars	Honey (as necessary)	Caution with all sugars, especially corn and fructose sweeteners
2. Artificial and herbal sweeteners	Stevia, Stevia Plus	Aspartame, saccharin
3. Fruit	Green apples, berries, avocados, Fresh coconut, grapefruit, lemons, limes and other citris fruits, and their juices.	Minimize bananas and melons. Avoid processed juices. Babies do not need to drink juice. Dried fruits in bulk storage bins run a high risk for fungal contamination.
4. Meat	Virtually all meats, including fish, poultry and beef and even breaded cuts. Grass fed beef is best.	Farm raised and grain-fed mean corn-fed, so watch for this on the label, and be cautious.
5. Eggs	Yes, all eggs are allowed	Avoid egg substitutes.
6. Dairy	Yogurt (especially goat yogurt) Gouda cheese, cream cheese, unsweetened whipping cream, sour cream made from real cream, butter, goat's milk, organic, hormone free cow's milk.	Avoid margarine, which is not a dairy product, and *trans* fatty acids.
7. Vegetables	Eat lots of fresh, unblemished vegetables and freshly made vegetable juice. Yams and legumes (beans and peas) are fine, as are potatoes when eaten in moderation.	Corn and corn products should be minimized for life. Mushrooms are fungi, NOT vegetables.
8. Beverages	Bottled/filtered water; non-fruity, herb teas; Stevia-sweetened, fresh lemonade or lime-ade. Sparkling mineral waters are excellent. Green tea is good for you.	Coffee and tea should be drunk sparingly. Sodas remain excluded, as do most sports drinks, which are high in sugar.

LifePhase (continued)

Food Groups	Foods that are ENCOURAGED	Foods that are DISCOURAGED
9. Grains	Oats (oatmeal), rice of any kind, quinoa, amaranth, millet, buckwheat, barley, flour tortillas, Sourdough bread. Aside from oats and rice, pasta likely remains the best source of grains, because scientists maintain you filter out mycotoxins when you drain the boiled water.	Grains, organic or otherwise, should be eaten in moderation, especially when they come in the form of yeast-raised breads. This is true regardless of whether the grain is "whole" or not.
10. Yeast Products	None.	Try to avoid mushrooms, alcohol, fermented soy products and yeast breads. Also, try to avoid foods that list yeast as an ingredient.
11. Vinegars	Unpasteurized, apple cider vinegar is best to use in dressings etc.	Caution with fermented foods such as pickles.
12. Oils	Olive, grape seed, flax seed etc. Use cold pressed oils when available. Omega 3 fatty acids are excellent when taken as supplements (flax seed, fish oils, evening primrose oil, shark liver oil etc.)	Partially-hydrogenated ("trans") oils, corn and peanut oil
13. Nuts	Raw nuts, including pecans, almonds, walnuts, cashews, pumpkin seeds and sunflower seeds. These are great snacks. Almond and cashew butters are excellent replacements for peanut butter.	Peanuts (and all peanut products) and pistacios are excluded, along with any obviously damaged or moldy nuts of the recommended sorts.

Kaufmann and Holland

Chapter 11
Popular supplements/ potent antifungals

In addition to the Initial Phase diet package laid out on the previous pages, Doug and I feel it necessary to touch on a few of the key supplements that have proved useful both in weight loss and in lessening the effects of problems that can often accompany weight problems, such as diabetes, heart disease and high cholesterol. Exhaustive textbooks exist that expound on every vitamin, mineral and herb that may be of use in treating these conditions. By all means, if you need more information than we have space to print here, you can find such books at your local bookstore or health food store. While we do advocate supplementation, we strongly urge you to stay away from both over-the-counter and prescription "diet pills," especially those containing ephedra.

Correct, sufficient nutrition is absolutely essential in maintaining a healthy weight. Although many dieticians continue to insist that eating a well-rounded diet provides this level of nutrition, this is just not true, for a variety of reasons. For example, vegetables grown in poor soil will always fall short of providing us with the nutrients we need.

I should take this opportunity to lay a popular myth to rest. Some of the people who promote supplements also push the "good old days" theory of health and diet. They do this in part to answer the question — *why are supplements necessary now, when a well-rounded diet used to be enough?* One good-old-days answer is that we are under a lot more stress now than our parents were. As plausible as that might sound at first, I'm afraid it just isn't true. Folks, Americans fought world wars beginning in 1914 and 1941. In between, we endured the Great Depression. Afterwards, we went through the red scare, faced the fear that the world would be eliminated by atomic bombs on a daily basis, and became embroiled in several more wars — one of which we actually lost. Throw in the Civil Rights movement and the assassinations of several prominent, American leaders, and you've got one stressful century. And that's not even looking at the final 30 years of it.

The real myth isn't the reasons that are derived from the good-old-days mind set. The real myth is the good old days, *themselves.* You see, when doctors said way back when that a well-rounded diet was enough, they were *wrong.* Food itself has never provided so many nutrients — and so much of them — that supplements couldn't have helped improve a given individual's health. We can talk about the "good old days" until we're blue in the face, but the fact remains that supplementation is not just a good idea *now.* It would have been a good idea *a hundred years ago.*

Ironically enough, even today your doctor may not have discussed with you the benefits of taking supplements. She may even have advised against them. "Show me someone who takes vitamin supplements," goes the standard line, "and I'll show you someone with very expensive urine."

If you really want to know how your physician feels about supplements, ask her the question: "Do you take supplements, Doctor?" I say that because of a cardiology seminar I heard about recently. One of the speakers asked an audience of heart specialists whether they recommended their patients take supplements that contain vitamins A, C, and E, and zinc and selenium. About a third of the doctors raised their hands. The speaker then asked the group, "How many of *you* take such supplements?" At that, *all* of the doctors in the room raised their hands. The point is, regardless of whether they recommend them to their patients, the vast majority of health care providers take supplements themselves.

The nuts and bolts of it are as follows: in order to get the broad range of elements required to enable enzymes and to create the chemical pathways for rejuvenation, you need to take supplements. Also, keep in mind that many of the vitamins, minerals and other substances described throughout the remainder of this chapter owe their disease-fighting capabilities to their documented, antifungal properties.[1]

Chromium picolinate

Dr. Gary Evans published a book in 1996 extolling the benefits of taking chromium picolinate,[2] only to have his work countered by medical reports as to the dangers of this mineral. In point of fact, the chromium found in chromium picolinate is a trace mineral that our bodies must have. In addition, the link between its deficiency and diseases such as liver necrosis in mice, muscular dystrophy and heart necrosis in minks, and liver dystrophy and muscle degeneration in pigs has been well known for years.[3]

In our bodies, chromium is found in highest concentrations in the outer layer of the kidney, the pituitary gland, the liver and the pancreas, where insulin is produced.[3] Many scientists believe that chromium both improves the efficiency of the insulin our bodies produce, and that it corrects our blood sugar levels. It achieves this second objective whether blood sugar prior to supplementation was too high, as with diabetes, or too low, as with hypoglycemia.[2]

The link between diabetes and chromium was first suspected in the medical field in 1977. A patient had been on intravenously administered nutrition for some time. The drip fed into her bloodstream happened to lack chromium, and she ended up developing severe diabetic symptoms, including nerve damage. Her doctor was able to reverse these symptoms by adding chromium to the drip.[4]

Dr. A.V. Costantini's research group has researched several of the studies that show how chromium acts against fungi, how it inhibits aflatoxin production by *Aspergillus,* and how it lowers blood LDL levels, the bad variety of cholesterol.[1] "The beneficial effects of chromium *re*pletion," he says, "are now so well established and the **trivalent** form is so free of toxicity that it should now be used in clinical medicine for the benefit of those suffering from atherosclerosis."

A 1997 placebo-controlled study in the journal, *Diabetes*, supports the finding that chromium lowers blood sugar, cholesterol and HbA1C. Low levels of this last element, or hemoglobin A1C, indicate that patients are succeeding in controlling their blood sugar levels over the long term.[5] In fact, the 1997 article emphasized that chromium supplementation had "significant beneficial effects" in lowering these numbers. Despite this, you will find that chromium is flat out omitted when you visit the American Diabetes Association (ADA) website and click on the nutrition and [recommended] supplements page.

It's difficult to understand why the ADA drops the ball on this and other therapies available to diabetics that cost much less than the heavily researched drugs produced by the pharmaceutical companies. Of course, much of the $170 million plus the organization raises every year does come directly from such companies.[6] Although we can see why the drug companies would have little interest in a cheap, over-the-counter supplement, we expect better from a nonprofit organization dedicated to eradicating diabetes. It looks as though a little more oversight of charity-based research organizations might be a good idea.

Opponents of chromium picolinate tend to make vague references to studies that show chromium can cause DNA damage that leads to cancer. Unfortunately, because of the way malpractice works, the average health care provider tends to remember very little about nutrition and lots about the cancer scares that occur from time to time.

So, is there a connection between chromium and cancer?

Certain studies do suggest that *hexavalent* chromium of the type used in industry may be a contributing factor in lung cancer. Although hexavalent chromium is indeed toxic, exposure to it is highly unlikely. Not only that, the kind of chromium in supplements is of the trivalent form, not hexavalent. Finally, the daily, recommended dose of trivalent chromium picolinate falls in the microgram range. It takes a million micrograms to make a single gram, which is about what a paper clip weighs. The levels of *hexavalent* chromium to which lung cancer victims were exposed were much higher.

Doctors generally recommend a daily intake of trivalent chromium that ranges from 200 micrograms (mcg) to 1200 mcg, divided up into two or three doses.[2]

Chromium and pregnancy

Incidentally, chromium studies have been performed with pregnant women who had developed gestational diabetes. The women's blood sugar levels stabilized at healthy levels. And, their babies were born problem-free. Keep in mind, diabetic women who fail to control their blood sugar levels during pregnancy run much higher risks of having children with birth defects.

Prudence should always be practiced. If you are trying to lose weight, simply keeping track of how you feel in the first few days and weeks of chromium supplementation should be enough. On the other hand, if you have diabetes, you should keep in very close contact with your physician. It also wouldn't hurt to start with lower doses, like 100-200 mcg a couple of times per day with meals.

Another warning to diabetics: one possible side effect of combining the Initial Phase diet with chromium supplements is an abrupt drop in blood sugar. That's why you need to stay in close contact with your doctor. If you are indeed on meds for diabetes, your dosage will need to be reduced to keep your blood sugar in a normal range.

We should review what happens when blood sugar is too low. You may feel irritable at first, and then agitated. Your hands may shake, and your heartbeat may speed up. If this should happen, in line with what your doctor or nutritionist has no doubt advised, you should down some fruit juice or eat an orange to raise your blood sugar to acceptable levels. Remember, if your blood sugar drops too far, you could pass out and even fall into a coma.

If you have impaired kidney function or are on dialysis, extremely low doses of most any medication or supplement should be used, if any. Kidney failure impairs the ability for your body to filter out a variety of drugs and supplements. Accumulation of these in your body can be dangerous, so please talk with your doctor if you fall in this category.

Coenzyme Q10

Despite its name, Coenzyme Q10 (CoQ10) counts as a member of the vitamin group. In fact, biochemically speaking, all vitamins are coenzymes, and vice versa. Practically speaking, however, some years ago scientists decided to stop admitting new vitamins such as CoQ10 to what seemed to be a never-ending list.

CoQ10 is of most value in heart disease and congestive heart failure, where it has been found to be more heart-protective than the pharmaceutical drug Captopril.[7]

Captopril falls in the ACE-inhibitor class of drugs commonly used in congestive heart failure. Doctors often prescribe ACE-inhibitors for their diabetic patients because the drugs seem both to delay the onset and to slow the progression of kidney disease.

In the study comparing CoQ10 with Captopril, 60 mg of CoQ10 per day were used, versus 37.5 mg of Captopril. It and numerous other, controlled studies have been made that similarly confirm the superiority of CoQ10. So, you should consider adding it to the medications that you may already be taking.

Marked improvement has been seen in the heart conditions of patients taking between 100-150 mg of CoQ10 per day.[7] Again, the substance's benefits are so well-documented — with a noted lack of side effects — that every patient walking in or out of a cardiologist's office should be taking it.

Magnesium

Magnesium deficiencies have been reported in heart disease patients, especially those with atherosclerosis.[1] Such deficiencies are potentially caused by mycotoxins. Not only that — magnesium has been shown to work directly against the fungi that produce mycotoxins in the first place.[1] Certainly, cardiologists and electrophysiologists are sold on the benefits of magnesium in preventing sudden death due to irregular heartbeat, or arrhythmia. Although magnesium is a mineral, there do seem to be more benefits to taking it than just electricity.

Specifically, because magnesium can also directly relax blood vessels, which in turn lowers blood pressure, the mineral is ideal for treating hypertension. At the very least, the water pills often prescribed in order to lower blood pressure can deplete our bodies of magnesium,[7] so it would be wise to take a magnesium supplement to offset this loss. Most authorities recommend that heart disease patients take on the order of one gram (1000 mg) twice daily, provided kidney function is normal.

Magnesium is one mineral that can have adverse effects in high doses. Taking huge, oral doses of magnesium will likely cause diarrhea. In addition, excessive levels of magnesium in the bloodstream can lead to over-relaxation of the muscles. Remember, both the diaphragm, which forces air in and out of the lungs, and the heart are muscles! If your kidneys have failed, your doctor will advise you against taking magnesium unless you specifically demonstrate a deficiency in your bloodstream. Your kidneys cannot get rid of excess nutrients when they are not functioning properly.

Hawthorn berries (*Crataegus oxycantha*)

Hawthorn berry is another supplement used primarily for conditions such as congestive heart failure. It has been recognized by many countries, including the United States, in being able to: dilate the peripheral arteries (in the arms and legs, thereby reducing the stress on the heart); increase oxygen utilization by the heart; mildly dilate the heart blood vessels (improving oxygen flow to the organ); and increase enzyme metabolism in heart tissue.[8] Most patients take between 100 to 250 milligrams (mg) of the 10 percent procyanidins solid extract, three times a day.[7] In studies of patients with Class II NYHA heart failure (New York's Heart Association assigns a classification of between I-IV to the severity of heart failure patients have suffered), hawthorn berry produced a marked decrease of heart rate, blood pressure, and other parameters used in studying and monitoring heart failure.

L-Carnitine

L-carnitine is a "nonessential" amino acid that our body synthesizes from the amino acid lysine. It has been thoroughly studied in regard to both heart failure and diabetes. Experts suggest a gram twice daily, more for diabetics.[7] This dose reduced the heart rate, cholesterol, edema and requirements for digitalis in patients studied. All of these results benefit congestive heart failure patients. In type 2 diabetics, L-Carnitine has been shown to increase the metabolism rate of blood sugar.[10] The amino acid is available as a prescription under the name of Levocarnitine[10] — and if it's a prescription, it must be safe (smile)!

Garlic

Daniel Mowrey, Ph.D. tells us that research on both animal and human subjects has irrefutably proved garlic's ability to lower cholesterol.[8] Garlic's ability to lower blood pressure and kill fungi is also well-documented. In fact, garlic destroy more than *200 species* of fungi. In addition, garlic can prevent DNA damage induced by mycotoxins such as aflatoxin, and even prevent *Aspergillus flavus* fungus from producing the mycotoxin in the first place.[1] Once again, the usefulness of a powerful antifungal such as garlic in treating high cholesterol and atherosclerosis confirms the intimate link between fungi and heart disease. Those of you reluctant to eat garlic and onions can find whole garlic supplements in capsule form.

Vitamin B1 (folate)

Folate is available in both over the counter and prescription forms. Folate is sold as a prescription mainly because of its ability to lower homocysteine levels in our bloodstreams. Elevated levels of homocysteine have frequently been found in people with heart disease. Folate seemed to help decrease these levels. Patients with the lowest folate levels have demonstrated a 69 percent higher risk of dying from heart disease, when compared with those with the highest levels.[11] So folate does seem to at least offer significant protection. The question is, how?

To answer this, K. Uraguchi described in a 1969 article how mold-contaminated rice can cause heart failure. In the 1940s and 1950s, Uraguchi and other scientists isolated the mycotoxin produced by this moldy rice. They called it citreo-viridin, from the *Penicillium citreo-viride* mold.

It so happens that thirty years earlier, improved inspection of rice and weeding out moldy samples had reduced the incidence of heart disease and deaths caused by this mold toxin. In the 1920s, doctors started to recommend vitamin supplements. It turned out that vitamin B1 — our friend folate — is effective in reducing the toxicity of citreo-viridin to the heart. To recap, mycotoxins cause heart failure. And, vitamins such as folate protect against mycotoxins. Connect the dots, and you arrive at the reason why folate supplements decrease our risks of dying from heart disease.

Although it might be more effective to simply eliminate mycotoxin-laden foods from our diets — ala the Initial Phase diet — in general this is close to impossible in practice. This reality makes taking a daily vitamin containing folate a worthwhile practice.

Multivitamins

When you think of a multivitamin, you probably picture a well-rounded supplement that contains vitamins, minerals, herbs and other "neutraceuticals." Given that our soil is sometimes depleted of minerals and nutrients, and given that many vitamins and minerals are excellent fungus fighters,[1] taking a multivitamin is definitely a good idea. There is a minus involved, however. We have seen a number of clients remain sick despite investing literally thousands of dollars a year in supplements. It's difficult to say why this happens. In practice, however, we've found that it's not what you give patients that improves their conditions, but what you take away from them. So, for the first two weeks after starting our Initial Phase diet, we have often recommended that patients refrain from taking supplements, except for the most necessary ones and those used specifically for their antifungal properties, such as olive leaf extract. People with heart conditions may choose to continue taking Co-Q10, while diabetics might want to stay on just chromium picolinate.

Very often dysbiosis, or alteration of the normal terrain of the bowel, needs to be corrected before taking a good, foundational supplement should be resumed. The general opinion of medical professionals today is that taking a multivitamin, multi-mineral supplement just makes sense. Ultimately, they are a lot like home insurance. Your home may be sturdy and capable of withstanding a great deal of abuse, but the rare disaster that comes along will make those insurance payments worth the expense.

1. Costantini, A.V. Fungalbionics Series: Etiology and Prevention of Atherosclerosis. Johann Freidrich Oberlin Verlag. Freiburg, Germany. 1998/99.

2. Evans, Gary, Ph.D. Chromium Picolinate: Everything you need to know. Paragon Press. Honesdale, PA. 1996.

3. Haper, H.A., et al. Review of Physiological Chemistry, 16th ed. Lange Medical Publications. Los Altos, CA. 1977.

4. Jeejeebhoy, K.N., et al. Chromium deficiency, glucose intolerance, and neuropathy reversed by chromium supplementation in a patient receiving long-term total parenteral nutrition. Am J Clin Nutr 1977;30: 531-538, as discussed in Nutritional Science News, Feb. 1999.

5. Anderson, et al. Elevated intakes of supplemental chromium improve glucose and insulin variables in individuals with type 2 diabetes. Diabetes, Vol 46, Issue 11;1786-1791.

6. Charity Navigator.org. Number quoted is for fiscal year 2001.

7. Micromedex.com, under AltMeDex Protocols. 10/2002.

8. Mowrey, D. The Scientific Validation of Herbal Medicine. Keats Publishing, Inc. New Canaan, Connecticut.

9. Rosenbaum, M. Super Supplements. Penguin books, New York, NY. 1987.

10. Mercola.com. 1999.

11. Modica, P. Folate linked to risk reduction in heart disease. Medical Tribune, Vol. 37, No 13., July18, 1996.

Chapter 12
Intelligent Exercise

All of the information in this book is for naught if you do not *exercise*. After all, God gave us arms and legs so that we could move. Such movement is never more important than in the effort to lose weight. So, it's time to get going, especially if you believe you may run an even higher risk for developing diabetes or heart disease than your weight problem would indicate.

Before you go out and spend your money on a pair of track shoes, on a gym membership or on personal trainer fees, the mental focus you will need to make a lasting change in life-style must be in place. For what it's worth, years of experience tell us that if you fail to make those changes, weight problems will remain to haunt you for the rest of your life.

Most people make the decision to exercise based on their emotions, more than they do on facts. Fear is a big motivator. Many times we are scared into exercising because we believe we may die from a disease unless we change our ways. Or, we may exercise in order to impress someone we find attractive, to pursue a friendship with a friend or neighbor, to improve ourselves, or to prove a point — to ourselves or other people.

There is a stronger motivator than all of the above, however, one that will keep you moving long after you would otherwise have given up. All you need to do to tap this source of strength is to perform a simple exercise known as the deep knee bend. Once on your knees in a humbled, kneeling position, ask God for help. Release your problem to him, and ask Christ, who dwells in your heart, to help and guide you as you make the necessary changes to your life-style.

I have found that the deep knee bend works better than things like the nicotine patch for people trying to quit smoking. That's because no one can truly change without making the firm decision that from here on out, a new person will occupy your body. That new person does not smoke, or may walk around the block in the mornings, or perhaps drink bottled water instead of soda.

For down-to-earth, practical help online, I especially like to look at runnersworld.com. The site offers practical, unbiased, motivating help for people taking their first steps in a pair of exercise shoes to seasoned athletes preparing for their 50th marathon. I especially appreciate the fact that they offer training advice for the sake of improving your health, not for scoring in the singles game.

Once you have made the decision to change, you should select an activity appropriate for your condition. If you are under age 45 and have no health problems, you can probably choose just about any method of getting moving. If you believe you may have a problem, see your doctor for a checkup before you begin. Diabetes and heart disease are not called the "silent killers" for nothing, so if you suspect you may be at risk, make sure you are on top of your health situation before you begin a vigorous program.

If you suffer from severe arthritis, look into a water aerobics program. Water will make you nearly weightless — thus taking pressure off of your joints — but the resistance to movement the water provides will still raise your heart rate.

If you are not sure where to start, many athletic centers offer trainers capable of tailoring a program specific to your needs, based on your current fitness level. God also provides us with a rather convenient gym called the outdoors that he offers free of charge. Certainly, no matter where we live, we can usually find a good area to walk in, whether it be around the block, in a park, around the high-school track, or inside of a mall.

You might try setting your alarm and getting outside before everyone else struggles out of bed. This is not only a great way to start up your metabolism — it also supercharges your spirit and mind with the wonders of creation. We've found that the early morning light even brings out the beauty inherent in downtown neighborhoods.

What you invest in your endeavor is purely up to you, but a pair of walking shoes, which you probably already own, is really all you need to start with for most activities. Swimming obviously requires its own apparel. For biking, all you really need is a beginner's bike — and a helmet, of course. The more expensive bike models don't provide any more exercise. You pay the extra money for a lighter frame or a smoother ride, neither of which translates to a better workout. The point is, don't let equipment you lack become a barrier to getting your body moving.

Let's take a look at some of the recent research regarding the impact of exercise upon disease. If you are at particular risk of developing diabetes, a 2002 study has concluded that with life-style changes alone you can reduce that risk by 58 percent.[1] The typical life-style changes offered by the medical community at this time include a low-fat, high-carb diet. So, we believe you could reduce your risks even further if you were to instead combine a high-protein diet with the exercise programs addressed in the 2002 study.

The American College of Sports Medicine supports the use of both resistance training (weight training) and endurance (aerobic) training to the point of considering these as excellent therapies for the treatment of diabetes. Aerobic activities such as walking, biking, or swimming decrease blood pressure and lower important inflammatory markers such as C-reactive protein (CRP), as well.[2]

If you take insulin, you may need to monitor your blood sugar more closely, or schedule your exercise so as to not coincide with the times of day your blood sugar levels are their lowest. Otherwise, you risk dropping your blood sugar to unhealthy levels. For type 2 diabetics not taking insulin, the latest findings show that it is probably not necessary to test your blood sugar or urine ketones before, during or after routine exercise.[2] The American College of Sports Medicine, however, continues to encourage testing, especially if you are a professional athlete.[3]

The exercise programs addressed in most studies last between 20 and 30 minutes, and are performed at least four days a week. You can start out at 10 minutes if you need to, however. The goal is to get moving and get your heart rate up. A rough gauge as to whether you are doing too much is if you can not carry on a normal conversation while you exercise, say with your exercise partner. If that's the case, you may be doing too much too fast. Doing too much too fast is the most common reason people suffer from exercise-related injuries. It's also one of the leading reasons for not keeping a program going long enough to see its benefits. So, be careful, especially in the early going.

You can determine the maximum heart rate you should aim for during any exercise program by subtracting your age from 220. If you have diabetes or heart disease — and you have clearance from your doctor to begin exercising — you will probably only want to increase your heart rate to 55-79 percent of the maximum, recommended rate. For example, if you are 60, your maximum heart rate would be 160 beats per minute (220-60=160). If you also have diabetes or heart disease, you should probably not aim for more than 126 beats per minute (160x79 percent=126).[2] To get a rough measure of your heart rate, stop what you are doing and find your pulse on your wrist or neck. Count the number of times your heart beats for 6 seconds, and multiply this number by 10.

As your endurance improves, you can work your heart rate up to 85 percent of your maximum. These are only general guidelines, which means you should review them periodically with your doctor. Also, some medications will prevent your heart rate from increasing, skewing these numbers. You will be able to tell over time how much endurance you are building because your morning, resting heart rate will generally drop as you get in better shape. It is not uncommon for endurance athletes to have resting heart rates in the upper 40s to lower 50s.

If you are overweight or obese, or if you suspect you may be at risk for heart disease or diabetes, a number of experts recommend that you take an exercise treadmill test prior to starting a strenuous program. This recommendation applies to anyone over the age of 35 with diabetes, or men over the age of 45 and women over 55 with heart disease or risks of the same. A treadmill test will assess your baseline function and help your doctor recommend an exercise program depending on your performance. It may also identify existing, uncontrolled hypertension or a lack of oxygen to the heart (ischemia) that would only show themselves while you are in motion. High blood sugar, high blood pressure, chest pains, neuropathy (nerve damage or numbness and weakness), kidney failure, heart failure, headaches, and certain forms of diabetic eye disease all require immediate evaluation by your physician prior to exercising.[2,3]

Once you begin to lose weight, make sure you stay with the diet program, as well, and that you continue to take your supplements regularly. And, always remember what about your past life-style led to your weight gain in the first place, so make sure that you do not repeat those patterns. This last part is often the toughest, so much so that success requires divine intervention. Remember, God will be your greatest cheerleader if you honor Him with your humility.

For links to websites that offer quality supplements, please click on knowthecause.com.

1. Unraveling the Causes of Diabetes. Science. April 26, 2002. Vol 296. www.sciencemag.org

2. Stewart, K. Exercise Training and the Cardiovascular Consequences of Type 2 Diabetes and Hypertension: Plausible Mechanisms for Improving Cardiovascular Health. JAMA, Oct 2, 2002; Vol 288, No 13.

3. Sallis, R.; Massimino, F., eds. ACSM's Essentials of Sports Medicine. Mosby. St. Louis, MO. 1997.

Chapter 13
Prayer's role in weight loss

Today, most people seem to agree that weight problems can be "cured" through a proper diet combined with appropriate exercise. While the only truly effective diet is one that is antifungal, productive exercise plans can vary widely, so long as they include both weight training and aerobic elements.

Certainly, when you know both what your problem is and what you need to do to solve it, that's a positive development. But I should warn you that this kind of knowledge can come with a dark side. Because the cure for weight problems involves a life-style change, it's all too easy to believe that you could have avoided putting on too much fat in the first place, had you chosen to lead a healthier life-style from the beginning. This point may lead some people to conclude that, "I have only myself to blame for becoming fat."

Stop right there, because assigning *blame* solves *nothing*. Instead, you need to decide who is *responsible* for *losing weight*. The answer to this question is obvious — *you*.

While we're on the subject, in the same way, the most important step in fixing marital and other relationships is *not* deciding whose fault it is that everything has fallen apart. Rather, if *you* are the unhappy person, *you* must take full responsibility for doing what you can to fix the relationship. As it turns out, you cannot change other people, even when they happen to be members of your own family. You can only change *yourself.* Finally, there is a word for people who wait for things outside themselves to change so that they themselves can become happy, and that word is "victims."

Unfortunately, we do live in a world that spends a lot of time on the blame game. So, as often as not, blaming ourselves for our failures — instead of taking responsibility for achieving success in the future — is joined by "I need to perform penance by wallowing in guilt and self-pity." Needless to say, such wallowing is self-destructive. It also seldom encourages us to lace up a pair of track shoes for an early morning run, nor gives us the incentive to eat healthier food.

So, how do we break this cycle of blame and guilt, followed by wallowing in it, followed by still more blame and guilt? The answer is a spiritual one — hence the title of this chapter.

Think about it. If you're like a lot of people, you have no difficulty praying when unforeseen disaster strikes. The odds are also better than even that you are pretty good at offering prayers of thanks for the blessings you receive. But what about when you goof — when you lose your temper and hurt the people you love with words you don't mean, when you bend the truth so badly you almost can't find the way back to reality, or when sheer laziness or carelessness on your part prevents you from realizing a dream, or others from realizing their dreams? Generally speaking, we never retreat further inside our own perspectives than we do at such moments of intense guilt. When this happens, we lose the ability to ask for the help we need.

The same truth likely applies to how you feel when you look down at your own waistline, or when you read the results of the latest test your doctor has run. What I'm saying is, it's quite possible that, on some level, you have come to believe that you don't deserve help. After all, you are to blame for becoming fat, right?

As a matter of fact, even if you don't buy my philosophy about *responsibility* rather than *guilt*, a single truth cancels out the guilt in question and wipes it from the record — you are *God's creation*. That means that God loves you, and will always love you. Virtually every denomination out there believes this to be true. Think about perhaps the most famous of Bible verses — John 3:16. John didn't write "For God so loved the perfect people." Neither did he write, "For God so loved the pretty good people." He didn't even write "For God so loved the people who have managed to take good care of their bodies." John wrote that "God so loved the *world* that he gave his only begotten son to die for us, that whoever believes in him shall not perish, but have eternal life."

I'll leave the explanation of the second part of John 3:16 to people in the ministry. For my purposes, the first part of the verse says it all, regardless of what your faith may be — God loves you. Every single one of you. God loves you when you burst with joy, when you feel guilty, when you get angry, and when you screw up. God loves you even if you have difficulty fitting through your own front door. It doesn't matter whether *you* think you deserve that love or not, God loves you.

The practical application of this realization is twofold. One, God's love gives you instant, incredible value as a human being. It makes you worth saving, no matter how much to blame you may feel for your predicament. Two, God wants to help in that saving. In fact, if you're reading these words, consider yourself as already benefiting from that help. I say this because I believe that God has called me to provide people with accurate, medical information on how to combat diseases such as obesity and live life to its fullest. So, you see, even if you haven't specifically prayed for help with your condition, you're already on the receiving end of it.

Now, what are you going to do? It is my hope that you will pray. Pray for correct perspective, for serenity, and for the peace that passes all understanding. Pray for the strength and perseverance to stick to the diet and exercise programs outlined in this book, augmented with advice and strategies from your own doctor. Pray for those you love, for those you hate, and for an end to that hate. Pray for joy. Pray for hope.

Pray when you get out of bed in the morning and before you go to bed at night. Pray before each meal. Pray while you are driving your car. Make a habit of praying all the time.

When you do drop everything to concentrate on prayer, make sure you are comfortable. Breathe deeply and slowly. Focus on your breathing first. Follow that by focusing on your blood flow. Then, narrow in on the nerve endings in your toes and in your fingers. Finally, shift your focus outward. Imagine what people you know are doing at that particular moment. Imagine what people you have seen on television or read about are doing. Think about — a fisherman on a wind-tossed boat off the coast of Novia Scotia, worried if he's going to land a big enough catch for the day. Pray for him. Pray for specific people you know to be in need or suffering.

It's up to you. My point is, rather than conceive of creation in abstract terms, you would do better to put it in concrete terms, terms that expand your horizons. Pray for correct perspective as you perform this exercise — a perspective that frees you from guilt and the victim mentality, as well.

You may find reading once or twice daily from a book of devotionals to be helpful. Perhaps you have several, favorite hymns you could regularly sing aloud as you pray, to give your prayer a physical dimension that will increase your concentration. One of my friends reads a passage from Tyndale Press's One Year Bible. Some of the Bible's more historical passages may make better food for prayer than others, so if you use Tyndale's, you may want to make sure you include a separate, devotional passage. The point is, without some kind of structure to your prayer sessions, they may lack direction and end up being idle exercises in daydreaming and, even worse, self-recrimination.

The above are just a few thoughts on how you might use prayer. I'm not a professional minister, and certainly there are dozens and dozens of books available on prayer. I did want to touch on the guilt issues surrounding obesity, however, because I believe they are one of the major reasons people fail in their attempts to lose weight.

The remainder of this chapter lays out a few more snippets on the relationship between prayer and health that you may also find helpful.

Seven Verses on Prayer and Health

Mark 5:34 — Daughter, your faith has made you well. Go in peace, and be healed of your disease.

Matthew 6:25 — Therefore I tell you, do not worry about your life, what you will eat or drink, or about your body, what you will wear. Is not life more important than food, and the body more important than clothes? Look at the birds of the air; they do not sow or reap or store away in barns, and yet your heavenly Father feeds them. Are you not much more valuable than they? Who of you by worrying can add a single hour to his life?

Matthew 6:31 — So do not worry, saying, 'What shall we eat?' or "What shall we drink?' or 'What shall we wear?' For the pagans run after all these things, and your heavenly Father knows that you need them. But seek first his kingdom and his righteousness, and all these things will be given to you as well. Therefore do not worry about tomorrow, for tomorrow will worry about itself. Each day has enough trouble of its own.

Philippians 4:6-7 — Do not be anxious about anything, but in everything, by prayer and petition, with thanksgiving, present your requests to God. And the peace of God, which transcends all understanding, will guard your hearts and your minds in Christ Jesus.

Proverbs 13:4 — The sluggard craves nothing and gets nothing, but the desires of the diligent are fully satisfied.

1Thessalonians 5:17 — Pray continually.

Psalm 121:1-2 — I lift my eyes to the hills — where does my help come from? My help comes from the Lord, the Maker of heaven and earth.

Evidence that prayer works

A study performed at Duke University Med. Center found that patients who received alternative therapy following angioplasty were 25-30% less likely to suffer complications. Patients who received "intercessory prayer" had the greatest success rate.[1]

A Harris, Wisconsin study conducted a random, controlled trial of the impact of third-person, intercessory prayer on results achieved by patients admitted to the coronary care unit. The prayer group demonstrated 10 percent fewer scoring elements than the usual-care group.[2]

In a recent, double blind study, patients prayed for by others had 11 percent fewer heart attacks, strokes and life-threatening complications than the control group.[3]

Some 75 percent of the studies reviewed show a direct relationship between religious commitment and health results, including prevention of recovery from illness, depression and substance abuse.[4]

Final thoughts

Wherever I go, I talk a great deal about the importance of diet, exercise, and stress reduction. To achieve this third component of good health, I've always relied on prayer.

Prayer is incredibly portable. Unlike weight machines or exercise bikes, I can take it with me wherever I go. Prayer never runs out. I never have to refill it or come up with a co-pay to get more of it, and I never have to renew my membership plan.

On my morning runs, I pray about the events and meetings of the upcoming day. I give thanks for the blessings I've received, including my health. Often, in the late evenings, I sit outside, look up at the stars and pray about what happened that day, and about the future. I pray for my wife and kids as they deal with their own successes and struggles, and I pray for guidance to help me be a better husband and father to them. I focus on understanding that there is a larger plan in which my life plays an important role, and for the strength to align my goals with that plan.

When I pray, I feel shielded from the madness — good and bad — that happens during the course of a day's work. I am refreshed and ready for more. I feel relaxed and reassured, knowing that I don't have to face anything by myself.

I can say with full confidence that prayer has helped me to lead a healthier, happier life.

1. BBC News, 11/01/ 2001.

2. Apagar, B., MD. Intercessor prayer and patient outcomes in coronary care units. Tips from other Journals. American Family Physician. Feb 1, 2000. Archives of Internal Medicine. October 25, 1999;159:2273-8.

3. ABC News.com. Aug 13, 2001. Can Prayer Heal? Scientists Suggest Recovery may be the hand of God at work.

4. Anandarajah, G., Hight, E. Spirituality and Medical Practice: Using the HOPE Questions as a practical tool for spiritual assessment. American Family Physician. Jan 1, 2001.

Part Three
Supporting Material

Your Fungal Quotient

The following is the latest in a series of questionnaires Doug and Dr. Dave have used for the past 30 years. Based upon research concerning known, fungal risk factors, the questionnaire is used to assess the degree to which patients may have been exposed to fungi, and the odds that the microbes (or their mycotoxins) lie behind a given problem. A PDF is available on request.

Medical History

yes no

☐ ☐ 1. At any time in your life, have you taken repeated or prolonged rounds of antibiotics?

      If so, how long were you on the antibiotics, and for what conditions?

☐ ☐ 2. Are you allergic to any medications? Please specify.

☐ ☐ 3. At any time in your life, have you taken repeated or prolonged courses of steroids or cortisone-based pills? If so, for what?

☐ ☐ 4. Have you been diagnosed with fibromyalgia?

☐ ☐ 5. Do you have, or have you ever had asthma?

☐ ☐ 6. Have you been diagnosed with arthritis?

☐ ☐ 7. Do you have diabetes? Type I or Type II (circle please)?

☐ ☐ 8. At any time in your life, have you been treated for worms or parasites?

☐ ☐ 9. Have you traveled outside of the U.S.? When and where?

☐ ☐ 10. Have you ever had cancer?

      If so, did you undergo chemotherapy or radiation treatment?

☐ ☐ 11. Have you had ringworm, jock itch, fingernail or toenail fungus? (circle please)

☐ ☐   Do you suffer from any of these problems at present?

yes no

☐ ☐ 12. Have you ever been diagnosed with attention-deficit disorder (ADD or ADHD)? List any medications you are currently taking for this.

☐ ☐ 13. Had you spent time in or near construction sites when you became ill?

General health evaluation

☐ ☐ 14. Do you suffer from fatigue? Circle your energy level (10 is lowest).
　　　10　　9　　8　　7　　6　　5　　4　　3　　2　　1

☐ ☐ 15. Do you often feel irritable?

☐ ☐ 16. Do you often feel dazed or "spaced out?"

☐ ☐ 17. Do you suffer from memory loss?

☐ ☐ 18. Do your muscles, bones, or joints bother you? (circle all that apply) Would you describe them as aching, weak, stiff, or swollen? (circle please)

☐ ☐ 19. Do you get more than the occasional headache? How long has this been so?
　　　a. What type have you been diagnosed with (migraine, tension etc.)?
　　　b. How many days a week do you get headaches?
☐ ☐ 　c. Do they feel as though they might be caused by a hormone imbalance?
　　　d. What medications do you take for your headaches?

☐ ☐ 20. Do you have itching, tingling, or burning skin? (circle please)

☐ ☐ 21. Do you have hives, psoriasis, dandruff, or chronic skin rashes? (circle please)

☐ ☐ 22. Do you have acne?

☐ ☐ 23. Are you on medications for the above skin problems? Name them, and how long you have taken them.

☐ ☐ 24. Do you suffer from hair loss?

☐ ☐ 25. Do your inner ears itch?

☐ ☐ 26. Does your vision blur for no apparent reason?

yes no

☐ ☐ 27. Have you been diagnosed with high or low blood pressure? (circle please)

☐ ☐ 28. Have you been diagnosed with high cholesterol or triglycerides? (circle please)

☐ ☐ 29. List medications you take for blood pressure, cholesterol or triglycerides. Include how long you have taken them.

☐ ☐ 30. Do you have mitral valve prolapse, a racing pulse or an uncontrolled heart beat? List medications you take for this condition, including how long you have taken them.

☐ ☐ 32. Have you ever been diagnosed with an autoimmune disease? Specify the disease, including when you were diagnosed.

☐ ☐ 33. Are you bothered by recurring problems with your digestive tract such as bloating, belching, gas, constipation, diarrhea, abdominal pain, indigestion, or reflux? (circle please)

List any medications you take for your condition, including length of dosage.

☐ ☐ 34. Have you taken multiple prescriptions of antibiotics for a chronic infection?

Describe the infections, including their duration and frequency.

☐ ☐ 35. Does your health problem get worse in response to heat? For example, does a shower, bath, or very hot weather make it worse? (circle please)

☐ ☐ 36. Do your symptoms worsen on damp days, or when you spend time in musty/moldy environments?

☐ ☐ 37. On days when the mold/pollen count is elevated, do you feel worse?

☐ ☐ 38. Do you often feel more unhappy than "normal" for a given situation?

☐ ☐ 39. Have you been diagnosed with depression?

☐ ☐   a. Are you presently seeing a therapist for depression?

b. List any medications you take for depression, including how long you have taken them.

yes no

☐ ☐ 40. Do you drink alcohol?
      a. How many times a week do you usually drink?
      b. How much do you drink on these occasions?
      c. For how long have you drunk alcohol?
☐ ☐   d. Have you ever gotten drunk on a regular basis?

☐ ☐ 41. Do you smoke cigarettes?
      a. How many cigarettes a day do you usually smoke?
      b. How many years have you smoked?
☐ ☐   c. Do (or did) your parents or spouse often smoke around you?

☐ ☐ 42. Have you had sharp cravings for corn, peanuts, or sugar? (circle please)

☐ ☐ 43. Have you spent time on a farm? How long ago, and for how long?

☐ ☐ 44. Has your home or office ever had a mold problem?
☐ ☐   Has either ever been flooded to any degree?

Allergies

☐ ☐ 45. Do you suffer allergic reactions to pollens, molds, animal dander, dust, mites, perfumes, chemical, smoke, or fabric store odors? (circle please)

46. List any allergy injections, and the length of time on them.

☐ ☐ 47. Are you allergic to any foods?
      a. Have you had food allergy tests run?
      b. Were these skin tests or blood tests? (circle please)

For women only

☐ ☐ 48. Are you 1)currently taking or 2)have you ever taken birth control pills? (circle please)
☐ ☐   Have you suffered complications as a result? Describe them.

☐ ☐ 49. Have you experienced uterine, vaginal or urinary tract problems such as endometriosis, polycystic ovarian syndrome or fibroids (circle, specifying if not listed)?

yes no

☐ ☐   50. Are your ovaries, thyroid gland, adrenals or pancreas malfunctioning? (circle please)

51. Among the following symptoms of possible, hormone disturbances, circle all you have experienced: PMS, menstrual irregularities, loss of libido, infertility, sugar cravings, weight problems, and often feeling hotter or colder than is normal for a given situation.

☐ ☐   Are you on medications for any these problems? List them, and the length of time for which you have been taking them.

For men only

☐ ☐   48. Do you now—or have you ever—suffered pain in the testicles unrelated to trauma?

☐ ☐   49. Have you ever been bothered by prostate problems?

☐ ☐   50. Are your testicles, thryoid gland, adrenals or pancreas malfunctioning? (circle please)

☐ ☐   51. Among the following symptoms of possible, hormone disturbances, circle all you have experienced: loss of libido, infertility, impotence, sugar cravings, weight problems, and often feeling hotter or colder than is normal for a given situation.

☐ ☐   Are you on medications for any of these conditions? List them, and the length of time for which you have been taking them.

We'd like to give you an exact risk assessment for X number of "yes" answers. The problem is, things aren't quite that simple. For example, say you answer "no" to every question above, with the exception of a "yes" for being on antibiotics for six months at one stage of your life. That one "yes" — combined with a weight problem — would suggest to us that you should get on the Initial Phase diet for at least a couple of weeks, in addition to following our Antifungal Program.

Having said the above, in our experience, more "yes" answers do tend to indicate a more serious degree of fungal infection and/or exposure to mycotoxins.

A Week of the Initial Phase Diet
Example menus

Initial Phase differs so much from what the average American eats that we've gotten a lot of questions as to what a menu based on the diet would look like. The layout below is not meant to be followed verbatim. And, remember, *Initial Phase* almost always requires more than a week to achieve results. Please note the emphasis on water, and refer to our recipe section/website for details on certain dishes.

Monday
Breakfast:	Fried eggs, uncured bacon, ½ grapefruit
Snack:	Almonds, water (always bottled or filtered)
Lunch:	Tuna with celery. Herbal tea
Snack:	Carrot sticks, water
Dinner:	Steak, steamed veggies, sparkling lime water
Dessert: (optional)	Plain yogurt with raspberries

Tuesday
Breakfast:	Omelet with onions, leeks, parsley, and chopped bacon
Snack:	Celery sticks, water
Lunch:	Chicken salad with Phase I dressing
Snack:	Cashews, water
Dinner:	Salmon fillets with lemon and butter, avocado salad
Dessert: (optional)	Green apple

Wednesday
Breakfast:	Poached eggs, freshly squeezed carrot juice
Snack:	Walnuts, water
Lunch:	Broccoli chicken without rice, herbal tea
Snack:	Grapefruit, water
Dinner:	Steak, spinach salad with lemon juice and olive oil dressing
Dessert: (optional)	Plain yogurt with chopped pecans and fresh cranberries

Thursday

Breakfast:	Scrambled eggs with breakfast steak
Snack:	Green apple wedges, almonds, herbal tea
Lunch:	Tuna salad with lettuce
Snack:	Broccoli, cauliflower, water
Dinner:	Halibut with sautéed vegetables
Dessert: (optional)	Yogurt with fresh blueberries

Friday

Breakfast:	Freshly squeezed carrot juice, hard boiled eggs
Snack:	Celery sticks or green apple wedges with almond butter
Lunch:	Beef patties, steamed and buttered asparagus
Snack:	Sunflower seeds, water
Dinner:	Kaufmann's favorite meal (see recipes)
Dessert: (optional)	½ grapefruit

Saturday

Breakfast:	Omelet with green onions, bacon, spinach leaves
Snack:	Carrot sticks
Lunch:	Cucumber salad w/ onions, tomatoes, black olives, olive oil
Snack:	Pecans, yogurt with blackberries, water
Dinner:	Steak with steamed broccoli
Dessert: (optional)	Sautéed green apples and cranberries with roasted pecans and whipping cream

Sunday

Breakfast:	Freshly squeezed carrot juice, ½ grapefruit, poached eggs
Snack:	Pumpkin seeds, water
Lunch:	Salad with grilled tuna, herbal tea
Snack:	Celery sticks, water
Dinner:	Stir-fried chicken, broccoli, snow peas, squash with butter
Dessert: (optional)	Almonds, chamomile tea

Recipes for the diets

Kaufmann's Favorite Meal

Dice: tomatoes, onions, cucumbers, avocado, and black olives.
Add: hard-boiled eggs and either smoked salmon or cubes of beef purchased from a health food market.
Toss: Add two tablespoons of olive or grape seed oil and the juice from a fresh-squeezed lemon as the dressing.

Spinach Salad

1 bunch spinach, torn or sliced to desired size	1 cucumber, sliced
1/2 to 1 cup cauliflowerettes	6 radishes, sliced (opt.)
1 - 2 stalks celery, chopped	2 eggs, hard-boiled & sliced

Toss together all ingredients. Flavor as desired with herbs and spices. Serve with lemon and oil dressing. Fresh sprouts or 1/4 cup roasted sunflower seeds may be added to give extra crunch.

Nine Vegetable Cocktail

1 pint fresh tomatoes	1 green pepper, sliced
1 cucumber, sliced	1 lettuce leaf
1 radish, quartered	a few sprigs parsley
1/4 onion, sliced	1 stalk celery
1 slender carrot	1 pint ice cubes, to desired consistency

In an electric blender, blend together all ingredients, adding ice cubes a few at a time. If juice freezes, allow to run a little longer before adding remaining ice. Add salt and pepper or other herbs and spices to taste. Increase ice for colder or thinner juice. Makes 1-1/2 quarts.

Almost Tartar Sauce

1/2 cup green onions, tops included, coarsely chopped

1 tsp. sea salt

1/4 tsp. pepper

1/4 to 1/2 tsp. Mrs. Dash

1/4 cup parsely, no heavy stems, coarsely chopped

1/4 cup cucumber, finely chopped

juice of 1/2 to 1 freshly squeezed lemon

1 tsp. capers

1 pint plain yogurt

Combine all ingredients except yogurt in a bowl, tossing to blend. Feed mixture through a meat grinder using the coarse blade, or use a blender on 'chop.' Stir results into yogurt. Chill.

Serve with fish, or with slices, chunks, or cubes of any vegetable.

Basic Vege-yogurt Dip

1/2 c. plain yogurt

sea salt to taste

spices and herbs as desired

juice of 1/2 lemon

Spices and herbs might include garlic, chives, marjoram, or thyme. Mix together all ingredients. Chill and serve.

Herb Dressing

1 tsp. dry mustard

1 tbsp. fresh parsley, chopped

1 tsp. dill weed

1/2 tsp. sea salt

1/4 tsp. tarragon

1/4 tsp. freshly ground, black pepper

pinch thyme

1/2 cup virgin olive oil

pinch oregano

Stir together all ingredients except olive oil until dry mustard is dissolved. Allow to sit for ten minutes. Blend in olive oil, beginning with 1/3 cup and adding additional oil to taste.

Use to dress green salads or serve with slices, chunks, or cubes of any vegetable.

Mexican Relish

1 lb. tomatillos, peeled	1 clove garlic
2 pinches cumin	2 serrano chilis
1/2 onion, minced	1/2 tbsp. butter

Blend together all ingredients. Melt butter in a skillet. Sautee mixture until onions and tomatillos are clear. Serve with chicken, fish, or other vegetables. Store leftover relish in the refrigerator.

Salad Dressing and Vegetable Marinade

1/2 cup olive oil	1 tsp. oregano
juice of 2 lemons	1 tsp. garlic powder

Mix together all ingredients in a pint jar. Fill jar the rest of the way with water. Shake well to mix, then pour over whole, sliced, chunked or chopped vegetables. Squash, radishes, cucumbers, broccoli, carrots, bell pepper, cauliflower, and onions work well. Refrigerate, allowing to marinate two hours or longer. Add other herbs and spices to taste.

To use over spinach or lettuce, add just prior to serving.

Curried Cauliflower

1 - 2 cups cauliflowerettes

1 onion, thinly sliced

1/2 cup fat-skimmed chicken stock

1/2 tsp. butter

1 tsp. curry powder, or to taste

1/2 tsp. cumin (opt.)

Combine ingredients in a small pan, cover. Simmer until most of the liquid has evaporated.

Variation: Other vegetables may be "curried" in this manner.

Deviled Eggs

6 hard boiled eggs, halved lengthwise

paprika to taste

2 tsp. dry mustard

2 Tbsp. plain yogurt

salt and pepper to taste

Separate yolks from egg whites. Mash yolks together in a small bowl. Add remaining ingredients, mixing well. Refill egg whites with yolk mixture. Arrange on a platter and sprinkle with additional paprika.

Beef Patties

1 lb. ground beef

1/2 tsp. sea salt

1/8 tsp. garlic powder

1 cup onion, finely chopped or 2 tsp. dried onion

1/4 tsp. black pepper

Mix together all ingredients. Shape into six patties. Broil or grill to desired doneness.

Variation: Ground chicken, turkey, or lamb may be used in place of beef. If lamb is used, add a pinch of oregano.

Chicken Stroganoff

1 lb. chicken, chopped or ground

1 med. onion, chopped

1 clove garlic, minced

1 cup chicken broth

1 tsp. sea salt

1/4 tsp. pepper

1/2 tsp. thyme

fresh parsley, chopped

2 Tbsp. olive oil

Heat oil in a wide frying pan over medium to high heat. Lightly brown the chicken. Just as chicken begins to brown, add onion and garlic, stirring until onion becomes limp and translucent. Add broth, salt, pepper, and thyme. Simmer, stirring frequently until thickened. Serve with brown rice. Garnish with fresh parsley.

Fish Fillet Almondine

2 lbs. fish fillets (snapper, cod, sole)

1/4 c. olive oil or butter

3 Tbsp. slivered almonds

1 Tbsp. lemon juice

1/2 tsp. garlic salt

1/4 tsp. pepper

Heat 2 Tbsp. oil in large skillet. Add almonds and sautee 2 to 3 minutes, stirring constantly until golden brown. Remove almonds and set aside. In remaining oil, cook fish 3 to 4 minutes on each side until fish flakes when pierced with fork. Transfer to warm platter. Add lemon juice, salt, pepper and almonds to pan drippings; spoon over fish.

Lemon-Fried Chicken

1 fryer chicken, skin removed

1/4 c. fresh lemon juice

1/4 tsp. garlic salt

3/4 tsp. sea salt

1/4 tsp. marjoram

1/8 tsp. pepper

1/2 tsp. grated lemon rind

2 Tbsp. butter

1/4 tsp. thyme

Cut chicken into serving pieces and place in a large, shallow pan. Mix together the remaining ingredients, except the butter. Pour mixture over the chicken pieces and marinate in the refrigerator for at least three hours, turning occasionally. Drain chicken on absorbent paper.

Preheat skillet, add butter. Add chicken and cook for 15 minutes with lid partially on. Turn chicken and continue cooking for 10 minutes with lid partially on. Place cover on tightly and cook for 15 minutes more. Total cooking time is 30 minutes.

Mexican Fish

1 - 2 lbs. fish, whole or fillets

1 clove garlic, freshly chopped

1 lime, freshly juiced

pepper to taste, white or black

1 small onion, chopped

1 lb. peeled tomatillos (Mexican green tomatoes)

2 pinches cumin

1 clove garlic

1/2 onion, minced

2 serrano chilis (opt.)

Pierce fish on each side with fork. Rub garlic into fish, pour fresh lime juice on inside and outside of fish, then sprinkle with pepper.

(continued on next page)

Marinate two hours. Place, with chopped onion, in cold skillet that maintains an even temperature. Leave on medium heat eight minutes, turn fish over, and cook until done, approximately ten minutes more.

Blend together remaining ingredients. Heat in separate skillet until onion and tomatillos are clear. Pour onto warm platter and top with cooked fish.

Note: this recipe contains no salt. The garlic and lime make it unnecessary.

Old Fashioned Pot Roast

3 lb. lean brisket of beef

1 clove garlic, minced

1/2 tsp. black pepper, coarsely ground

1 large onion, chopped

1 small bay leaf

1/2 tsp. sea salt

a variety of vegetables, cut into pieces

Preheat oven to 450 degrees. Rub meat with garlic and pepper; place in a greased Dutch oven or heavy saucepan. Brown for 10 minutes on each side.

Slowly and carefully add 1 cup water and remaining ingredients. May also add cleaned, cut vegetables such as carrots, celery, bell peppers, or rutabaga for a simple, one dish meal.

Reduce oven temperature to 300 degrees. Cover and bake 3 hours or until tender.

Makes approximately 10 servings.

Turkey Salad

1 cup turkey, cooked and diced

2 cup rice, chilled

1 cup celery, diced

1 medium-sized, green pepper, shredded

2 Tbsp. parsley, chopped

1/2 c. olive oil

1/3 c. lemon juice

1/2 tsp. curry

1 Tbsp. pimento, chopped

Mix together turkey, rice, and vegetables; chill. Combine oil, lemon juice, and curry; let stand for 1 hour. Pour dressing over salad just before serving.

Tuna Salad

1/2 c. plain yogurt

1 Tbsp. lemon juice

1/4 tsp. sea salt or Mrs. Dash

1 jalapeno pepper, chopped (optional!)

1 12-oz. can tuna, crumbled

1 small onion, sliced

1 stalk celery, coarsely chopped

Lightly blend all ingredients. Chill and serve with slices, chunks, or cubes of any vegetable.

Makes approximately 1-1/2 cups.

An excerpt from Doug Kaufmann
and David Holland's
Infectious Diabetes

• •

Chapter 2:
An Overview of the Problem

Let's begin by building a foundation for the remainder of our discussion. Following an overview of what happens in diabetes and how the disease is treated, we'll take a critical look at part of the stance standardized medicine has taken. Not coincidentally, this analysis will offer further support for our own arguments concerning diabetes.

How do our bodies process sugar?
Eating sugar — and carbohydrates, which are quickly broken down into sugar — causes the pancreas to release insulin into the bloodstream. Insulin is produced by beta cells, which are located inside the pancreas's islets of Langerhans.

Cells throughout the body respond to insulin by acting to absorb the rise in sugar. When the sugar in the bloodstream drops back underneath a given concentration, the pancreas tapers off its production of insulin, and sugar absorption slows.

How does diabetes impact this process?
Type I

In Type I, or juvenile, diabetes, the body turns against and destroys its own, insulin-producing beta cells. Scientists believe that an immune system malfunction is to blame, which is why they classify type 1 diabetes as an autoimmune disease. They theorize that, for reasons that remain unknown, victims' immune systems have mistaken the beta cells for invading viruses or bacteria. We will introduce data that disputes the "autoimmune" theory in chapter six.

With the destruction of the beta cells, insulin production becomes impossible. Without insulin, cells cannot absorb sugar from the blood stream, sugar that they need for energy. Exhaustion kicks in. As blood sugar skyrockets, the kidneys spin into overdrive to do what they can to filter out the excess, just as they would any other substance present at levels greater than healthy. This leads to an unquenchable thirst and frequent bathroom trips. It can also mean unexpected weight loss. Kidney overdrive is an imperfect fix. Blood sugar levels remain as much as two times higher than normal, a condition that can lead to much more serious consequences over the long term. Not coincidentally, the word "diabetes" was coined to describe the high sugar content of ancient, diabetic patients' urine. Hyperglycemia, or high blood sugar, is another term often used.

The medical world has yet to develop a cure for type 1 diabetes. The standard method of coping with the disease is through replacement of the lost, human insulin through daily or even more frequent injections, and a low-fat diet designed to minimize cardiovascular complications in the future. Regardless as to how successful diabetics are in regulating their blood sugar levels, the odds remain overwhelming that they will develop the disease's complications. Those include blindness, kidney failure, heart disease, nerve degeneration and gangrene that necessitates the amputation of a limb.

Type 2

Damage to the pancreas and a corresponding lack of insulin play little if any role in type 2 diabetes. The problem lies instead with the body's cells in general, all of which depend upon insulin in order to absorb sugar. For reasons unknown, their sensitivity to the hormone drops dramatically. In fact, blood sugar levels remain high despite the presence of up to *five times* the normal level of insulin. Researchers have labeled this resistance to insulin as "Syndrome X," or "Metabolic Syndrome."

As with type 1 diabetes, type 2 forces the kidneys to work overtime. Type 2 also shares many of type 1's other symptoms, including the frequent need to urinate, constant thirst, exhaustion and sudden weight loss. The weight loss involved is usually more than made up for as the disease progresses. Because Syndrome X deprives cells of the sugar they require, the same cells refrain from telling your brain when you've had enough food. The absence of such a signal makes it easy to overeat.

How do we know if we should be tested for diabetes?

The American Diabetes Association (ADA) recommends that everyone over the age of 45 has his or her blood sugar level tested once every three years. Because of the nature of the disease, there are additional warning signs that could make the test a good idea even if you are younger.

Seven warning signs that you should be tested for diabetes

1. You suddenly feel tired all the time.
2. You seem to be almost constantly thirsty.
3. You feel the need to eat even though your stomach is full.
4. You've recently lost weight without dieting.
5. Your vision blurs for no apparent reason.
6. You get frequent headaches.
7. You feel a numbness or a tingling in your hands and/or feet.

All of these signs can be triggered by something else besides diabetes. Even if you display most of them, that is only an indication that you should see your doctor for testing, not that you have actually developed diabetes.

The first test

If the warning signs are there, your doctor may perform what is called a random plasma glucose test. Plasma is the liquid portion of blood, while glucose is basically the same thing as table sugar. This test can be given at any time, regardless of whether you have had anything to eat recently. If the results show greater than 200 milligrams (a fifth of a gram, or a little less than 1/4 teaspoon) of sugar per deciliter (a tenth of a liter, or about 1/2 cup) of blood, your doctor will likely schedule you for a fasting plasma glucose test. Incidentally, 200 milligrams of sugar just barely sweetens a deciliter of drinking water.

The second test

The fasting plasma glucose test requires that you've had nothing to eat and nothing to drink besides water for at least eight hours. Results of less than 110 mg/dl — roughly half the concentration of sugar allowed for the first, random test — mean that something else is causing your symptoms besides diabetes. If you are over the age of 45 and simply following the ADA's recommendation that you be tested, a result of less than 110 mg/dl means you have nothing to worry about.

Results between 110 and 125 mg/dl indicate that you may have what is called "impaired glucose tolerance" or "insulin resistance" — one step away from diabetes and a major warning that you should change your life-style before it's too late. Experts estimate that as many as a third of all Americans are insulin resistant.[6]

Results of 126 mg/dl or greater generate a preliminary diagnosis that you have developed diabetes. According to the ADA, 90-95 percent of all cases of diabetes are of the type 2 variety.

The third test
If you test at 110 mg/dl or greater on the first, fasting plasma glucose test, your doctor will likely schedule you for the same test a second time a few days thereafter, to reconfirm that you have developed insulin resistance or diabetes.

Progress checks
If you are diagnosed with diabetes, when you go in for your regular checkups your doctor will likely order one of two tests in order to see how well you have been controlling your blood sugar. The HbA1c (Hemoglobin-A1c) evaluates your efforts over the last three months. A result of 7 percent or less means you pass. An at-home version of the HbA1c has become available, for which you prick your own finger and mail in a blood sample. Test results are available as soon as a week later. Another test termed the *fructosamine*

assay generates your average blood sugar levels over the last three weeks.

What is the standard treatment for diabetes?

Type 2 diabetes is managed through drugs that do one of four things. Biguanides make cells more sensitive to insulin, which in turn stimulates them to absorb sugar present in the bloodstream. Biguanides also suppress the release of sugar into the bloodstream from the liver. Alpha-glucosidase inhibitors work in the small intestine to prevent the enzyme alpha-glucosidase from converting starch into sugar. Thiazolidinediones act directly upon the body's energy-starved cells, increasing their sensitivity to insulin. Finally, sulfonylureas and meglitinides cause the pancreas to release more insulin.

The above drugs can generate heavy side-effects, including headaches, weight gain, increased cholesterol and triglyceride counts, bloating, diarrhea, stomach cramps, flatulence, liver damage and a lower white blood cell count. The thiazolidinedione Rezulin was banned in Europe when a patient taking it died of liver-related complications.

Type 1 diabetics rarely take the above medications. Instead, they inject themselves with insulin, usually twice a day. Insulin comes in four, basic types, which vary in their speed of release from immediate acting to 24-hour release.

About a third of type 2 diabetics will eventually require insulin, as well. In addition to managing diabetes through drugs, the standard of care for diabetes recommends a low-fat diet and a regular, exercise routine. Diet and exercise have been shown to decrease the need for medication.

The hole in standardized medicine's approach

Let's take a critical look at standardized medicine's reasoning as to how diabetes develops in the first place, and its prognosis as to how likely it is that diabetics will suffer from the disease's complications.

The American Diabetes Association tells us that what we eat has zero to do with whether or not we develop diabetes. The organization also maintains that, regardless of how well they control their blood sugar levels, a third of all diabetics will suffer complications. As mentioned above, these complications include blindness, kidney failure, cardiovascular disease and gangrene requiring amputation of a leg or an arm.

The ADA's first position appears to be firmly grounded in logic. For example, about 90 percent of America's 17 million, type 2 diabetics are at least 20 percent overweight. That's a fact. Now, it stands to reason that you're going to see a wide variety of eating habits in a group composed of that many people. So, it's easy to agree with the ADA. Seventeen million diabetics can't all be all eating the same, wrong thing. The problem *has* to be that they are simply eating *too much*. So, it must be true — the content of our diets doesn't lead to diabetes. Instead, eating too many calories and carrying around excess body fat cause the disease.

Problem: If half of America is overweight, and 20-30 percent of the country is clinically obese, then we're missing between 60 and 110 million diagnoses of diabetes. Put another way, if simply overeating *anything* causes diabetes, then how have millions of overweight people escaped the disease?

Some mainstream medical practitioners sidestep this question. They point to the indications that several million undiagnosed and borderline diabetics live in America alone. In other words, millions of the overweight haven't escaped diabetes, they just have yet to be diagnosed. Don't buy this maneuver. While it may be true that several million people remain unaware that they have diabetes, the notion that 100 million diabetics are walking around undiagnosed is a bit hard to swallow. Perhaps even more importantly, millions of overweight and clinically obese people *have* had their blood drawn, only to test *negative*.

To sum things up, some overweight people get diabetes, but most do not. And, almost ten percent of type 2 diabetics are *not* overweight. So, overeating *anything* doesn't explain the situation. How on earth does standardized medicine fill in the gap?

Aha! some of you are saying. The answer must be — *genetics*! In fact, the world has never seen a more powerful tool capable of explaining just about anything to just about everyone. Elementary school teachers teach us about the monk Mendel and his hobby of crossing tall and short pea plants. Later, we study Darwin and natural selection. We go on to jot down our family medical histories every time we see a new doctor. By that point, we believe that we are destined to display the same weaknesses as our parents and grandparents have, whether we like it or not.

We *don't* read about the studies of twins who have grown up apart. In those studies, though they certainly still appear *identical*, each twin's medical history demonstrates a *different* susceptibility to disease. That's just one example from a growing bank of evidence that, with regard to health, the *habits we learn* from our parents often carry more weight than the *genes we inherit*.

Scientists employ a technique called *Occam's razor* in evaluating theories. Occam tells us that, all things being equal, the simplest explanation of a set of facts is usually the correct one. Let's try the razor on the standard line of reasoning concerning diabetes. In order to say that the kind of food we eat plays no role in whether or not we will develop diabetes, mainstream medicine brings in two props. The first one reads that millions upon millions of people have yet to be diagnosed with the disease. The second one reads that the reason countless more millions of overweight people will never get diabetes is that they are genetically programmed not to. Got your razor handy? Cut those two, convoluted props to shreds and watch the *it can't be the food* theory collapse in on itself.

If twins who grow up apart display different levels of vulnerability to diabetes, while twins who grow up together — eating the same things — do not, it has *got* to be the food! Moreover, its very simplicity *ala* Occam makes the *diet causes diabetes* theory a good one.

The odds are that you already believe as much, if you are reading this book. You may even believe that, with a combination of a diet designed to control blood sugar levels and exercise, *anyone* can beat diabetes. In fact, a number of recent books beg to differ with the standard line on diabetes in saying just that. Blindness, kidney failure, heart disease and amputations can all be avoided.

Not so fast. It takes more than a few slashes of Occam's razor to generate sound theory. Remember, a third of all diabetics who dutifully control their blood sugar levels will *still* suffer from the complications of diabetes. That's like saying a third of all alcoholics who never drink again will somehow still be locked up for DUI! This tells us that the high levels of sugar in the blood cannot be the only reason diabetics develop complications. There must be another factor at work.

Once again, *genetics* could certainly be that factor, but as the studies of separated twins show, it is overrated as a universal, one-size-fits-all explanation. Plus, not only is genetics is the ultimate cop-out scientifically, it convinces a lot of people to throw in the towel when they still have a fighting chance. After all, why change your life-style if the final outcome is preordained?

Let's review our position thus far: *diet causes diabetes.* Let's go ahead and expand that to, *something we ingest* — including medicine, food, water and even air — *causes diabetes.* That formulation explains how a third of all diabetics could still be in danger of developing complications, even after maintaining stable blood sugar levels over the years. Although they have controlled the key symptom, they have yet to deal with the mechanism that caused their disease to begin with. All things being equal, the odds are that the same mechanism is generating the complications, as well.

We have come to believe that microbial fungi are the mechanism in question. In chapters to follow, we will lay out the evidence that implicates them — and the mycotoxins they produce — as the cause behind diabetes and its complications. Subsequent to this argument, we will introduce a comprehensive program of diet, supplements and exercise designed to stabilize blood sugar, neutralize fungi and their toxins, and reduce future exposure to a minimum.

Prescription Antifungals

Some information courtesy <u>The</u> <u>Sanford</u> <u>Guide</u> <u>to</u> <u>Antimicrobial Therapy, 13th</u> <u>edition,</u> 2000, ed. by Gilber, D. et al, Antimicrobial Therapy, Inc., and the Tarascon Pocket Pharmacopoeia, 2002. Tarascon Publishing

Quite often, Doug and I have found it necessary to advise clients to use prescription antifungals in addition to the natural antifungals discussed earlier.

Just as certain antibiotics are called for treating specific, bacterial infections, certain antifungal drugs are indicated in treating their respective, fungal illnesses. Most, however, are called "broad spectrum" because they kill a variety of fungi without regard to genus or species.

With the exception of some older medications such as nystatin, most antifungal drugs tend to be very expensive. Diflucan (fluconazole) 200 mg tablets, for example, can go for more than $12 a pill, while the newer, intravenous, lipid forms of amphotericin can sell for as much as $1,000 per day of treatment.

With the major exception of the rigid, cell wall that fungi possess in place of the flexible, cell membrane in human cells, fungi and human cells are similar. So, designing drugs that will kill fungi but spare their human hosts can be costly and time-consuming. Furthermore, new drugs have to be discovered constantly because fungi — especially *Candida albicans* — gradually become resistant to the old ones. The research and development factor keeps the price tag on antifungals high. The vulnerability of chemotherapy and AIDS patients to fungal infections — and risk of dying without the drugs to fight such infections — makes them especially effected by the high cost of antifungals.

On the Medscape website, John Rex has cited a study by M. D. Anderson that indicates *Candida krusei* and *Candida tropicolis* have surpassed *Candida albicans* as causes of blood stream yeast infections.[1] These non-albicans *Candida* are generally resistant to Diflucan (fluconazole) and have become prominent due to widespread use of the drugs to curb yeast infections in cancer and AIDS patients.

Antifungals for both internal and external use exist — powders and creams for skin infections, and pills, suspensions, and injections for internal use. Infection type dictates treatment. For example, athlete's foot (*tinea pedis*), jock itch (*tinea cruris*) or simple dandruff can be treated with over-the-counter creams, powders, sprays, or shampoos that contain antifungal chemicals. In contrast, other external infections such as ringworm of the scalp (*tinea capititis*), extensive or large areas of ringworm of the skin (*tinea corporis*), and toenail fungus (onychomycosis, or *tinea unguium*) require oral antifungals that penetrate the skin and nail bed. Examples of such medications include griseofulvin, Lamisil, Nizoral, Diflucan, and Sporanox. The FDA has not designated Lamisil and Diflucan for treating skin or nail infections, respectively, but the drugs have commonly come to be used for these situations, to great effect. *Tinea versicolor*, a fungal infection that commonly causes spots of decreased pigmentation on the skin, responds equally well to both topical and oral antifungals.

Internal infections require internal antifungals. These, again, may come in the form of liquids, pills, capsules, or intravenous doses. Nystatin represents a broad-spectrum antifungal that is really not even absorbed into the blood stream, although it is taken internally.[2] So, nystatin is perfect for intestinal fungal infections. Doug and I have found nystatin to be useful for many conditions, especially bowel diseases including Irritable Bowel Syndrome, ulcerative colitis, Crohn's disease, gas, cramps as symptom of yeast gas production, diarrhea, and constipation. Although nystatin is actually a mycotoxin produced by a soil fungus, it is one of the safest drugs on the market, having no drug interactions and basically no side effects other than possibly a little nausea when taken in high doses. If you do feel ill after taking nystatin, it is more than likely not the drug, but rather the 'die-off effect,' or Herxheimer reaction, that the drug has caused. In this, a large amount of dead and dying fungus is somehow released suddenly into patients' bodies, making them feel as though they have the flu. The good news is, if you do suffer and then recover from a die-off reaction after taking an antifungal drug, it's pretty strong proof that fungi were, in fact, resposible for causing your condition to begin with. Remember, determining the cause of a given problem is often more than half the battle.

Amphotericin B and Diflucan may be used to treat serious fungal infections in hospitalized patients. These drugs are administered intravenously. Diflucan may also be taken orally for outpatient treatment of less serious, though bothersome, infections such as thrush (infection in the mouth and sometimes throat), vaginitis and cystitis (bladder infection). Some of the newer formulations of amphotericin have lessened the side effects of this drug, which had led to the older formulation's nickname, "Amphoterrible." Despite its notoriety, it remains one of the few drugs capable of tackling serious, deep-seated fungal infections such as zygomycosis. Untreated, zygomycosis can kill an immune-compromised person within mere hours.

Nizoral and Sporanox are chemically related to Diflucan. These two drugs are useful against systemic infections of blastomycosis, histoplasmosis, coccidioidomycosis, sporotrichosis, paracoccidi-oidomycosis, and phacohyphomycoses.[3] Sporanox may be used for some cases of aspergillosis, although amphotericin B is more often used for more serious infestations.

Antifungal drugs can be classified as fungicidal or fungistatic, depending on whether they actively kill fungi or just stop them from growing. Fungicidals include Nystatin, Lamisil, griseofulvin, amphotericin B, and some of the newer antifungals, such as Cancidas. Cancidas (caspofungin acetate) is a fermentation product of *Glarea lozoyensis*. The new drug is targeted at invasive aspergillosis in cases where amphotericin B proves to be either ineffective or too toxic. Medscape.com's John Rex tells us that, in its earlier studies, Cancidas was also found to be effective against *Candida*, *Histoplasma*, and *Pneumocysitis* species in mice.[4] According to the 2001 Merck & Company package insert with which it comes, Cancidas inhibits synthesis of Beta 1,3-D-glucan, a component in the cell walls of fungi. The corresponding loss of integrity causes such cell walls to leak, eventually killing the fungi altogether. Because our own cells are protected by flexible membranes instead of walls, we are prevented from suffering the same effect.

The remaining drugs available are fungistatic. Newer, diflucan-related drugs under study include voriconazole, ravuconazole and posaconazole. The hope driving the development of these new drugs is that we will be able to lessen side effects and, thereby, make safer drugs that are even more effective against previously resistant fungi.

While antifungal drugs are indeed very powerful and effective, like any other drug, they bring with them various side effects and drug interactions. Nystatin and Lamisil probably have the safest profiles. Please consult with a physician who is (or who would be willing to be) well versed in the benefits and risks of these drugs. Since prescriptive antifungals are, unfortunately, not used as often as antibiotics, many physicians and even pharmacists are a little rusty in their mental antifungal database. That is all right, though; I've always thought that the physician who doesn't refer back to his books is either extremely intelligent or overly egotistical; and I have met, and probably been, both of these.

1. Managing Fungal Infections in the New Millennium. April, 2000. Medscape.com.
2. Goodman and Gilman's Pharmacological Basis of Therapeutics, 1975.
3. C. C. Kibbler. Principles and Practice of Clinical Mycology. 1996.
4. Medscape.com, 2000.

Oral, systemic medications

Continuing our discussion of prescription antifungals, let's take a closer look at each of the individual drugs your doctor might prescribe for you.

Diflucan (fluconazole)

A fungistatic (inhibits fungal growth), oral antifungal, Diflucan is the only antifungal known to significantly penetrate the blood brain barrier and spinal fluids. It is used in the treatment of candidiasis (thrush, vaginitis, skin, bloodstream, meningitis, skin, etc.), coccidioidomycosis, and cryptococcosis, as well as some other infections for which FDA approval has not yet been obtained, including toenail infections. Some *Candida* species have become resistant to this drug.

Diflucan is 'category C' for pregnancy. A designation of 'A' would mean the drug is completely safe. Furthermore, mothers are advised not to take it while breast-feeding. Otherwise, Diflucan has a relatively good safety profile. However, treatment with any oral systemic antifungal carries small risks of liver toxicity and drug interactions. So, as when taking any medication, good communication with your physician remains essential.

While Diflucan gives good body fluid levels for the treatment of a variety systemic fungal illnesses, including urinary tract diseases, it can cost from $10-$19 for a single, 200 mg tablet. The drug comes in 100 mg pills as well as in suspension form (10 mg/ml and 40 mg/ml concentrations). Dosage must be adjusted according to your kidney function if you have kidney disease.

Lamisil (terbinafine)

Approved for treating toenail and fingernail fungal infections, Lamisil is also quite expensive, costing at least $6.50 per pill. On the other hand, the drug has the fewest side effects and interactions of all the systemic, oral antifungals. Lamisil also kills most fungi and yeast, although it is ineffective against *Candida albicans*. Dermatologists often use the drug for fungal infections of the skin, although this is not a FDA approved indication. Treatment for toenail fungus requires 12 weeks. This drops to six weeks for fingernail fungus. Maintaining a low carbohydrate diet will also assist in the treatment of any fungal infection.

Sporanox (itraconazole)

Indicated for the treatment of aspergillosis, candidiasis, coccidioidomycosis ("San Juaquin Valley Fever"), blastomycosis, histoplasmosis, sporotrichosis, pseudallescheriosis and paracoccidioido-mycosis, among others, including nail or skin fungal infections, Sporanox comes in capsules of 100 mg and a suspension form of 10 mg/ml. Better drug levels are obtained with the suspension form or when taking the capsule with an acidic beverage, such as a citrus drink. Sporanox is relatively expensive. Discuss drug interactions with your doctor. If you are taking any type of cholesterol-lowering drug, it cannot be taken with systemic oral antifungal medications.

Nizoral (ketoconazole)

Now available in generic form, the 200 mg strength of ketoconazole is not used for many infections, given the advent of newer and "cleaner" antifungal drugs. Nizoral may still be used for Chronic Mucocutaneous Candidiasis and *Tinea versicolor* (a skin fungal infection characterized by lighter or darker colored areas of skin in the infected areas) and ringworm infections that do not respond to topical antifungal creams. Nizoral also has been shown to lower PSA levels in men.[1]

Griseofulvin

One of the older, oral antifungals and still the treatment of choice for scalp fungal infections in children, griseofulvin has been replaced by Sporanox and Lamisil for the treatment of fingernail and toenail infections. Griseofulvin must be taken for long periods of time and yields lower cure rates than some of the newer drugs. Despite lack of FDA approval, many dermatologists use Lamisil in place of griseofulvin when treating skin and scalp fungal infections, citing the better safety profile and overall lower cost of the Lamisil treatment.

1. Medical Tribune, 01 May 1997.

Oral, organ-specific medications

Mycostatin, Nilstat (nystatin)

A broad spectrum, fungistatic (resticts the growth of fungus) and fungicidal (eliminates fungus) drug discovered by two researchers in the 1950s in Albany, New York (hence the name Nystatin, after New York State), this *intestinal antifungal* is not absorbed into the bloodstream to any significant degree and is therefore wonderful at attacking intestinal yeast. Nystatin is virtually free of side effects and drug interactions. No resistance patterns have been seen with yeast as of yet. The drug comes as a cream and powder for topical use. For internal use it is available in a suspension for children and tablets for adults. The suspension of 100,000 units/ml concentration is dispensed in a 60 cc bottle and is usually prescribed in amounts of 2 ml 2-4 times per day for infants through older children. The 500,000 unit tablets are prescribed in the amount of 2-3 tablets 2-4 times per day in adults. Nystatin is safe to take during pregnancy and while breast feeding.

Mycelex

Available in 10mg dissolvable "troches," mycelex, or clotrimazole, is poorly absorbed in the body but good for use in treating oral thrush (candidiasis). Typically one might dissolve one on the tongue five times per day for several days.

Topical antifungals

Most topical antifungal creams and powders can be obtained over the counter without a prescription. When conditions such as athlete's foot or jock itch fail to respond to such antifungals, this is an indication that a diet change may be in order, as well as a visit to the doctor for prescription strength medications, either topical or oral.

Intravenous antifungals

Diflucan (fluconazole) and amphotericin B (known as Fungizone, Amphotec, Albecet, and AmBisome), along with Cancidas (capsofungin), are all available in IV forms and are generally used to treat life-threatening, fungal infections in a hospital setting. Amphotericin B, especially in its older forms, is associated with numerous side effects, hence it's nickname "ampho-terrible." That said, the drug is relatively safe to take during pregnancy if needed (it is a Category B drug) and can be lifesaving in the event of serious fungal infections.

Newer antifungal drugs are being developed at this time and are focused on the treatment of serious fungal infections in patients whose immune systems have been weakened severely by cancer or by chemotherapy and other drugs. Systemic fungal infections in these cases can rapidly overtake patients, especially in the absence of aggressive treatment.

Kaufmann and Holland

Index

About
Dr. David Holland, M.D.

David Holland is president of North Texas Nutrition Consultants. He works with Doug Kaufmann and Mediatrition on a number of ongoing projects, including documenting the roles fungi and fungal toxins play in common, human illnesses, and communicating his findings to the medical community.

Dr. Holland holds a B.S. in Microbiology from Texas Tech University. Since obtaining his M.D. from Texas Tech University Health Sciences Center in 1993, he has worked in primary care, urgent care, occupational and nutritional medicine. He is a Diplomat of the American Board of Family Practice, as well as the American Board of Ambulatory Medicine.

Dr. Holland joined Doug Kaufmann in operating a nutritional medicine clinic in Dallas, Texas in 1996. He went on to complete his residency at John Peter Smith Hospital in Ft. Worth, Texas in 2002, and is currently Board Certified in Family Practice.

Dr. Holland is married with two children. He stays in shape by jogging and running in the occasional marathon.

About
Doug Kaufmann

Doug Kaufmann is a nationally recognized author, lecturer, television and radio show host, with more than 30 years of experience in diversified health care.

Kaufmann served as a Navy hospital corpsman in Vietnam, where he was honored with the Combat Action Ribbon, Vietnamese Cross of Gallantry and the Vietnam Service Medal, one bronze star.

After Vietnam, Kaufmann added an American Society of Allergy Technicians certification to the training he'd undergone in the Navy. While working in allergy/immunology with a Los Angeles specialist, he studied food allergies at the Washington University School of Medicine. He co-investigated several research papers with doctors at USC Medical School. Later, he opened a laboratory and staffed it with four, research immunologists focused on food and fungal research. Kaufmann's laboratory devised the first ELISA tests for food allergy, and it conducted significant research aimed at better understanding the food-disease link.

A group of Texan physicians recruited Kaufmann in 1987, having become interested in the laboratory technology he'd developed in Los Angeles. During subsequent studies in Dallas, many patients with various, apparently incurable diseases responded favorably to dietary changes and antifungal drugs.

Kaufmann began broadcasting his findings in nutrition on Texas radio in 1992. At one time, his "At A Glance" vignettes were broadcast daily by more than 200 radio stations.

Kaufmann transitioned to television in 1999, as the host of *Your Health with Doug Kaufmann*. Currently you can catch him on the nationally syndicated television program, *Know the Cause*.

Kaufmann's other books include *The Food Sensitivity Diet* (1984), *The Fungus Link* (2000), *The Germ That Causes Cancer* (2002), and *The Fungus Link Volume 2* (2003). Each book offers an alternative viewpoint to prevailing medical thought on the diagnosis and treatment of disease.

Currently, Kaufmann and Dr. Holland devote most of their time to research and writing, and holding seminars on their findings throughout the United States.

Kaufmann and his wife, Ruth, have been married for more than 20 years. They live with their two sons in a Dallas suburb.

Other books by Mediatrition

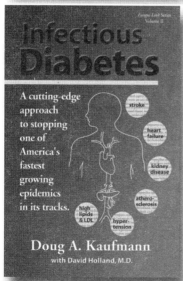

See knowthecause.com for details, please.